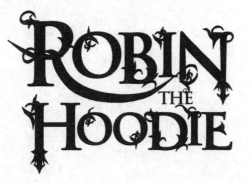

ROBIN THE HOODIE

An ASBO History
of Britain

MICHAEL O'MARA BOOKS LIMITED

First published in Great Britain in 2009 by
Michael O'Mara Books Limited
9 Lion Yard
Tremadoc Road
London SW4 7NQ

A CIP catalogue record for this book is available from the British Library.

Papers used by Michael O'Mara Books Limited are natural, recyclable
products made from wood grown in sustainable forests. The manufacturing
processes conform to the environmental regulations of the country of origin.

ISBN: 978-1-84317-396-0

1 2 3 4 5 6 7 8 9 10

www.mombooks.com

Designed and typeset by Ana Bjezancevic

Printed and bound in Great Britain by Clays Ltd, St Ives plc

CONTENTS

ACKNOWLEDGMENTS

The author would like to thank his wife Jennifer Hester, Hannah Knowles, Lisa Jackson, Ana Bjezancevic, the late Henrietta Marshall, his history teachers at Heathfield and tutors at St Peters, the Internet, coffee and nicotine lozenges, all of whom made this work possible.

*For Mum and Dad, who bought
me my first history book.*

INTRODUCTION

ONE SUMMER'S DAY WHEN I WAS A CHILD, I SAT READING a book of British history when a long shadow fell across me. I looked up and saw old Mr Asbosen from down the lane looming over me.

'You're wasting your time with that crap,' he growled. 'The real history of these isles is much more interesting: more fighting and drinking. We fought on the beaches! Drank on them too. One time I spewed off the top of Beachy Head… Come with me – I'll show you the only remaining true written record of British history. My ancestor wrote it. It's a family heirloom that's been handed down from father to son.'

I followed old Asbosen to his cottage, where he plonked

down a very old-looking tome in front of me. It contained the familiar stories of British history but not as I knew them. Antisocial skulduggery abounded. I was hooked, and that summer I spent many afternoons in Asbosen's cottage, lost in the world of his ancestor's stories.

When I grew up, I moved away but I still thought of the stories in Mr Asbosen's book. Last year, I determined to visit him and read them again. After a long journey, I arrived at his front door – only to be told by a kindly lady that he no longer lived there.

'No one's seen or heard of him for years,' she said. 'Some say he took to the road and is wandering the leafy lanes of England to this day.'

'Really?' I said sadly.

'No, not really,' she replied. 'He was taken away after they found him defacing history books in the public library and screaming that they were all wrong. Terrible thing. And he didn't have any trousers on.'

Asbosen and his book were gone – but that day I returned home and I began to write down as many of the stories as I could remember.

Chris Pilbeam

2009

Queen Boadicea's Big Night Out

ENGLAND HAS PRODUCED MANY GREAT MEN, BUT THE first true English hero was a woman: the warlike Boadicea.

The Ancient Britons were a striking race of people, always dressed head to toe in distinctive chequered clothing: the men spiked their hair with exotic gels and inked themselves with permanent designs of barbed wire and strange writing in foreign languages. All of them drank to excess, especially at sporting events, and, although the Romans had officially conquered them some years earlier, they were always ready for a punch-up.

Boadicea, the queen of the Iceni tribe, was the most wild of them all. The Roman historian Cassius Dio described her thus:

In appearance she was most terrifying. Her voice was great and harsh, a mass of bleached hair extensions fell to her hips and her vast gullet was capable of draining a flagon of mead in one gulp.

The Roman emperor Julius Caesar was wary of the Britons, and he decided to bring them to heel and make them into good citizens of the empire. One evening, a Roman emissary arrived at Boadicea's village with unwelcome news. He stood in the village square, cleared his throat and said, nervously:

'By the orders of the great and mighty Caesar, the troublesome and warlike customs of the Britons are to be stamped out immediately. This will start with a new dress code. Everyone will now dress like Romans and chequered clothing is outlawed as of midnight tonight. Where is Queen Boadicea?'

'Erm… she's gone to London,' someone said. 'For a girls' night out… in her best chequered gear.'

'Oh bugger,' said the emissary. He rode to London as fast as he could – but he was too late. Boadicea and a large contingent of ladies had already disembarked from their chariots at King's Cross dressed in full chequered regalia and were heading for the West End, tavern by tavern.

At midnight, the girls arrived at their first nightclub. Boadicea had consumed eight pints of watermelon-flavoured mead and was not amused when the Roman centurion on the door blocked her way with his arms crossed.

'Haven't you heard, love?' he said. 'Chequered gear is now banned. Orders of the emperor.'

'I see,' said Boadicea, and leapt on the man and sank her fingernails into his groin. The centurion called for back-up in a high voice but Boadicea's friends overpowered the bouncer-centurion and his legionaries and piled into the club, where they swiftly took advantage of a two-for-one offer on shots. The city garrison was alerted and came running, but Boadicea and her friends mistook the soldiers for strippers, debagged them to a man and forced their commander to gyrate on a table while they jabbed five-sestertii notes into his pants.

Next, they sent word to the rest of the Britons that their queen had been offended, adding that there was a two-for-one offer on shots. As Roman soldiers surrounded the nightclub to besiege it, the first Briton support unit arrived with a ferocious roar. Wielding swords, axes, bottles and road signs, they piled through the soldiers and rushed the doors of the nightclub without even pretending to form a line, drank the bar dry of two-for-one shots and then poured outside again to paint the town red. More and more Britons turned up, all of them bent on pillage, looting, massacre and pulling.

It was the most terrible spectacle ever witnessed, wrote Cassius Dio. *The Britons massed in the area known as Piccadillium, where they put innocent theatre-goers to the sword, burned refreshment stands, threw bricks at the soldiers of the emperor, copulated in the gardens of temples and placed a traffic marker on the head of the great statue of Caesar. When a legionary demanded they remove it, they beheaded him and pelted the corpse with kebabs. A great slaughter ensued, with thousands massacred. I myself was placed in a dustbin and rolled almost into the Thames, narrowly escaping with my life.*

In the middle of the chaos was Boadicea, wrestling with three burly legionaries who were trying to restrain her.

'I am fighting for my lost freedom,' she yelled, 'for my outlawed chequered hat, and because I am drunk!'

Shrieking wildly, she punched all three legionaries unconscious and staggered away to find a kebab. By now, the city was in flames and London's citizens were fleeing. Boadicea found a kebab shop, kicked the doors in and forced the terrified owner to make her the biggest kebab ever with extra chilli sauce *and* chips on top. Then, she wandered down to the Thames to eat it and watch the city burn.

This act was to prove her undoing. When the great roar of victory finally went up from the Britons, Boadicea sprang up

and lost her grip on the kebab. In trying to catch it, she lost her balance and fell into the Thames. Her heavy gold clown chain around her neck and billowing chequered tribal outfit dragged her to the bottom of the river, where she remains to this day.

Nothing was seen of Boadicea again, apart from a solitary chequered baseball cap that floated unnoticed down the Thames the next day. However, her vengeful spirit is said to dwell in Soho, occasionally mugging Italian students.

EMPEROR HADRIAN'S NEIGHBOUR FROM HELL

DURING THEIR TIME IN BRITAIN, THE ROMANS BUILT roads, forts and monuments that can still be seen today – but our most famous Roman construction is a wall. Hadrian's Wall stretches for seventy-four miles across Cumbria and Northumberland from the Clyde to the Forth and is the work of the emperor Hadrian, a man who, when not running an empire that spanned most of Europe, just wanted to relax and get on with people.

Hadrian was mostly based in London but he had a small holiday home in Northumberland. It wasn't a great palace – just a modest, ten-slave villa where he could go fishing or potter around his garden for respite from the business of empire. One Friday evening, he arrived at his villa very grumpy and cross from dealing with an insurrection in Palestine, only to find several caravans parked on the edge of his property. They belonged to the king of the Picts, the wild and warlike people who lived in Scotland. The king, a shaggy and rough-looking man, told Hadrian that he had just purchased the land and would be building several holiday chalets on the site.

Outwardly Hadrian was polite, but inside he was furious. He considered summoning his legions but decided he didn't want an all-out war with his neighbours. Instead, in the morning, he fetched some rocks from outside, which he placed along the boundary of his property next to the caravans. When he was done, he felt much better and laid down on his balcony for a nap. However, when he woke up much later, he felt that something was wrong. On closer inspection, he realized that the line of rocks had been moved several feet into his garden.

'That's it,' yelled Hadrian. 'Someone summon the legions.'

The 95th Legion was marched up from Chester and, with them as back-up, Hadrian went to the king of the Picts' caravan and thumped angrily on the door. There was no answer. He hammered again and decided to walk away.

'Mighty emperor,' said one of Hadrian's centurions. 'I hear giggling from within.'

Hadrian pressed his ear to the door; the centurion was right. He could hear whispering, giggling and someone saying 'Summon the legions' in a lisping, girly voice. Hadrian barked an order: a perfectly straight road was to be built to the nearest wood without delay, where his legionaries were to fell timber to construct a proper boundary fence.

The soldiers set to work and, by the afternoon, the fence was finished and painted white. Happy at last, Hadrian cracked open an amphora of wine and settled down in his favourite sunlounger with a knotted handkerchief placed on his head.

His peace did not last for long, though, for soon he heard a rhythmic thudding coming from behind the fence. He put down his crossword angrily and peered over the fence. There, kicking a football against it repeatedly, were the king's teenage sons. Suddenly, one of them hoofed the ball over the fence where it landed right in the middle of Hadrian's daffodils, flattening several of them. Rather than apologizing, the boys just asked for it back. Hadrian bit his tongue and returned it to them but no sooner was his back turned than the ball soared over again. This time it hit an expensive statue of the god Jupiter and knocked its nose off.

Angrily, Hadrian drew out his dagger and plunged it into the football, which he flung back over the fence. Now there was silence, and the stressed emperor decided to call it an early night and go for a long chariot ride in the morning.

Hadrian got up the next day feeling greatly refreshed and strolled down to his stables, where a terrible sight awaited him. Someone had scraped a key along the side of his red chariot and his horses were lying on the floor. They refused to get up and Hadrian noticed a white powder around their mouths. He dabbed a finger in it and licked it. His horses had been sabotaged with sugar.

Hadrian marched into his garden and fetched his hosepipe,

which he stretched all the way to the fence and poked underneath it into the king of the Picts' garden. He turned on the tap at full blast, fetched fresh horses, and went for his chariot ride, taking care to pull an almighty wheel spin in the king's new driveway to send gravel flying all over the place. When he returned from his drive, the king of the Picts was standing in the middle of a muddy lake, swearing foully. It was the beginning of a long and terrible feud that would last for months.

The most mighty emperor could hardly enjoy the use of his garden at all, recorded the chronicler Tacitus, *for every time he went outside the barbarian king would play music loudly or swear over the fence. On the Ides of March, the emperor found the word 'scum' written in mosaic upon his driveway; another time, his garden gnomes were arranged in lecherous and provocative positions. The only reprieve came when the barbarian king went to the tavern for lunch – on these occasions the emperor could sally forth into the enemy's garden and smear kitchen grease on the king's dustbin lids so that foxes and other beasts would spread the rubbish throughout the flowerbeds.*

Hadrian finally snapped one day when he woke to find a raiding party of Picts had rampaged through his garden and trampled his herbaceous borders. He could take no more.

'Summon the legions,' he cried. 'And some builders.'

He put his legions to work constructing a wall between the properties, stretching from coast to coast with a timber rampart six feet high and a fort full of soldiers placed at every mile. It was a long and arduous task, and the builders were harassed at every turn by the king of the Picts and his sons, who called them dreadful names. Work over-ran and there was a dispute over planning permission, but after six years the wall was complete and it ran from sea to sea across the top of England. Finally Hadrian could relax, and he enjoyed the peace and quiet of his villa for the rest of his days.

King Alfred and the Cakes

THE WISEST AND GREATEST KING OF SAXON ENGLAND was King Alfred, who people know as Alfred the Great. He built new towns across the land, drew up a new code of laws, created England's first navy and set up schools to promote learning. However, none of this would ever have happened if it hadn't been for Alfred's adventure with some cakes.

In the year 878, the fearsome, bloodthirsty Vikings attacked a West Country town: there were so many of them and they were so strong that the English were broken up and scattered and it was every man for himself. Alfred fled on foot into the wooded swamps of present-day Somerset. After a long day

of fleeing, he came upon an old, run-down woodcutter's hut
surrounded by strange, leafy plants, and he knocked on the
door. A sharp-featured old woman poked her head out of the
window.

'Are you the old bill?' she demanded, not recognizing the
bedraggled man before her as her king.

'No,' said Alfred. 'Just a weary traveller. May I please stay
here for the night?'

'Fine,' said the woman, taking pity on the dirty-looking
figure. 'You can stay,' she said, 'but you'll need to keep an eye
on these cakes I have cooking in the oven.'

'Can I have one?' said Alfred.

'No you cannot,' said the woman, rapping the king's hand
with a ladle. 'These are for me to sell.' And with that, she went
out to gather firewood.

Alfred looked around him. The hut was very strange.
It smelled of spices, its walls were decorated with curious
hangings and a set of bongo drums was piled in the corner.
The cakes began to rise in the oven and the smell made Alfred
feel very hungry. He took a peek inside the oven and they
looked good. After a while, Alfred could stand the temptation
no longer and grabbed a cake, which he wolfed down, and
then he lay down on a cushion to relax.

King Alfred felt very sleepy and a little strange. Then he felt terribly sick, as if blood were rushing to his head. He staggered outside and threw up in the odd-looking plants. These were now brightly coloured and seemed to move. A few minutes passed and Alfred began to feel better so he went indoors to think of a plan. However, this didn't work because all his thoughts kept moving. He gave up and sat down again.

Shortly the woman returned. The house smelled of burning and she looked in the oven to find the cakes black and smouldering. She turned around to find Alfred playing the bongo drums and staring into space.

'You ate one of the bloody hash cakes, didn't you,' she squawked.

'The what cakes?' mumbled Alfred.

'The hash cakes,' shouted the woman, picking up a broomstick. 'I needed to sell those. But they're in such a state only a ravenous Viking would eat them. How am I going to earn a living now?'

'Selling wood,' Alfred slurred.

'Right,' said the woman. 'Selling wood in a forest full of wood. You dipshit.'

'Woman,' said Alfred. 'I am your king. Bring me tea now. Also biscuits.'

At this point, the woman struck him very hard across the head with the broom.

When Alfred woke up it was morning and he felt very relaxed, although his head throbbed a little. He remembered vaguely that his royal dignity had been affronted but he couldn't quite recall why. As he was trying to piece the evening together, he heard a scream. The woman bolted through the front door of the hut from the garden and ran straight out of the back door with a screech of 'Vikings!' Alfred jumped to his feet and looked through the window. Fierce-looking, hairy men with axes had surrounded the hut.

'Come out, Alfred,' roared their leader. 'Come out and be slain!'

Alfred had to think swiftly.

'Very well,' he said. 'But you must be very hungry after all that massacring. Would you like some delicious cakes before you slay me?'

'Surely you mistake me for your plus-size mum,' growled the leader. 'Come out this minute and be slain!'

'Actually, we are quite peckish,' said one of the Vikings sheepishly.

'Fine!' shouted the leader, in a temper. 'Bring the cakes. We'll eat them and then cut you into pieces for the crows.'

Alfred reached into the oven and pulled out the burned hash cakes, arranged them nicely on a tray and took them outside. He was wrestled to the ground in an instant and sat on by a particularly large Viking, while his foes passed the cakes around and gobbled them down.

'Now,' said the Viking leader, 'prepare to... ooh.' He stared at his hand and slowly moved it back and forth. 'Ooh dear,' he said. 'I need to sit down.'

Before long, the Vikings were in a terrible state: several were rolling around in the swampy mud; some were giggling; others were being sick; yet others had started a bongo-drumming session. The big Viking who had sat on Alfred was now sitting in the branches of a nearby tree having a panic attack and accusing everyone of whispering about him.

By the afternoon, the Vikings had come to – yet, instead of killing Alfred in the most violent way possible, they sat around chatting peacefully. The old woman re-emerged from behind the house and brought them tea, for which they thanked her very politely. After some time, the leader got up and asked Alfred whether – if it was all right by him – they could stay here, since being out in the fresh air had done wonders for their bad tempers. After some thought Alfred agreed, and told them that they could start a village on the spot.

'You are a most wise and gracious king,' said the Viking leader. 'In your honour, we shall hold a festival every year on the anniversary of this day.'

'Sounds good to me,' said Alfred. 'Old woman – what is the name of this place?'

The old woman took a sip of tea. 'Glastonbury,' she said.

ETHELRED THE UNREADY: ENGLAND'S LEAST PREPARED KING

HERE IPSWICH WAS RAIDED AND ON THIS YEAR, IT WAS decided to pay tax to Danes for the great terror which they made by the sea coast. It would have been different if King Ethelred the Unready had turned up; yet, again, the dozy boy did oversleep and miss his carriage to the proceedings. He claimed that his alarm clock failed to go off but his Chancellor swore that he did walk past Ethelred's chamber in the middle of the night and heard the King watching cartoons online at very late an hour.

THE ANGLO-SAXON CHRONICLE, 991

King Ethelred came to the throne in the year 978 when he was just thirteen. Unlike his ancestor Alfred, he wasn't great.

The young Ethelred was not ready for kingship. In fact, he was rarely ready for anything at all.

Coronations during this period in time were lavish affairs. After the crowning, all the great men of the kingdom would swear their loyalty, after which the new king would give a speech before everyone had beer and cake. But at Ethelred's coronation, when he came to read out his speech, he stumbled over the first few words and then fell silent. A low murmuring went up in the hall, for many thought this was a bad omen for Ethelred's reign, and many others were just hungry for cake. As the murmurs grew louder, Ethelred's chancellor stepped up to help him read the speech – but the young king snatched the parchment away angrily.

'The first act of my rule,' shouted the young king, 'will be to do away with all coronation speeches in the future.'

'You will do no such thing,' said the chancellor to the young king, 'or your mother will be receiving a letter about you. Let me see your notes – I shall help you read your speech out.'

'Never,' snarled Ethelred, but the chancellor snatched them from him. The king looked down at the floor.

'There's nothing on this parchment, Majesty,' said the chancellor. 'Where is your speech?'

'I lost my speech,' said Ethelred. 'No, wait, I had it all written out, and then my little brother spilled a cup of tea all over it, so I ran to the palace kitchen for a cloth and when I came back, the royal hunting dogs had eaten it and messed all over it and everything.'

'You didn't do any notes at all, did you, Your Majesty?' said the chancellor. 'You stayed up all night pretending that you were working but you were just mucking around on the Internet. Weren't you?'

'Yes,' Ethelred whispered.

'Pardon?' said the chancellor.

'Yes,' Ethelred said more loudly. 'I won't let it happen again, sir.'

'You have deprived the nobles of the kingdom of their rightful cake,' said the chancellor. 'Now go to your bedchamber on your own and write the speech properly.'

Ethelred went upstairs and stayed in his bedchamber for a very long time, while the great men of the kingdom sat around glumly staring at the cake. At length, the chancellor relented and went upstairs to help the young king along. But when he pressed his ear to the door, the chancellor heard, quite clearly, the sound of videogames being played. Angrily, he burst in through the door to find the king sitting there in his pants, covered in crumbs and glassy-eyed from a three-hour VikingFighter3 gaming session. Sadly this was to be typical of Ethelred's entire reign.

One year England came under attack from the Danes, who would raid the coast in their longships and escape before Ethelred got it together to confront them in battle. Late in the summer, however, a messenger brought word that the Danes had now landed with a great army of warriors and were marching on London. A council of war was convened and it was decided that the English would meet the Danes in battle the next day, with Ethelred at their head.

The following morning the English strapped on their swords and chainmail and rode out solemnly to defend their city against the hordes. The two armies met in an Essex field and drew up their ranks, banging axes on shields and hurling insults at each other. But something was missing. There appeared to be no sign of the English king. The leader of the English army apologized to his Danish opposite and promised that the king would be there in fifteen minutes.

Two hours later, there was no sign of Ethelred and everyone was in a thoroughly foul mood. The Danes wanted to go to the pub and the English soldiers could be seen angrily looking at their sundials and shaking their heads. Suddenly a small figure on horseback appeared on the horizon. It was Ethelred. He was red-faced and out of breath but his army gave a great cheer.

But then they noticed that something was missing.

'Majesty,' growled the chancellor, 'where are your sword, armour and helmet?'

Ethelred coughed nervously.

'Couldn't find them,' he said.

'Speak up,' said the chancellor, loudly.

'Couldn't find them,' Ethelred sulked. 'I shall have to sit and watch.'

'You will do no such thing!' roared the chancellor. 'Bring forth the lost property chest!'

At this, a great peal of laughter went up from both sides, for this was a great dishonour.

'Not the lost property chest!' cried Ethelred. 'Everything in there stinks!'

'This is not a fashion show!' yelled the chancellor. 'Get digging in that chest or you will fight in just your pants!'

Ethelred reluctantly opened the chest and pulled out a fifty-year-old helmet, two left boots, a chainmail vest that smelled of wee and a non-branded sword that was three sizes too big. Reluctantly, he put it all on and waddled onto the battlefield to peals of laughter.

'I don't want to be king any more,' muttered Ethelred.

Sadly, he got his wish as he had failed to lace his boots properly. They came undone while he was in single combat with a Danish prince and he put down his shield to tie them back up. As a result, Ethelred lost his head and the English lost the battle, and as the chancellor was led away with his hands tied, it occurred to him that he really should just have made the king watch from the sidelines with the girls instead.

GLAMOUR GIRL GODIVA

ONG AGO, THE CITY OF COVENTRY WAS RULED BY AN earl named Leofric of Mercia. He was a powerful and greedy man who lived in luxury at the expense of the townspeople, whom he taxed harshly.

His wife was the beautiful Lady Godiva, who was as kind as her husband was cruel. It hurt her that the people of Coventry suffered so, and she would implore her husband to reduce the taxes, which kept them in poverty. Leofric ignored her pleas, usually because he was engrossed in playing online poker. He spent thousands of groats of tax money a year on this habit, playing late into the night, then falling asleep on his keyboard, only to wake up in the morning and start again. One day, however, Godiva lost her temper and unplugged the computer, which forced Leofric to take notice.

'Fine,' said Leofric. 'We shall play poker for it. If you win, I will lower the taxes, however, if you lose, you will stop nagging me.'

'Fine,' said Godiva. They sat down at the table and Leofric dealt a hand of poker. Godiva played well but Leofric's skills were too sharp, and before long, he had cleared her out of chips. Godiva was beaten – but she refused to give up.

'Double or quits,' she said.

'You've got nothing left to bet with,' said Leofric. 'Mmm… lots of taxes for me.'

'Strip poker!' cried Godiva.

'You're on,' said Leofric, with a crafty grin.

Godiva began well and within a few hands, Leofric had removed his boots, tunic and hose and was almost down to his ace-of-spades-patterned pants. But things started to go wrong. It was as if Leofric could see through Godiva's cards, for he beat her time and again. Very soon, she sat there in nothing but her long, golden hair, glaring daggers at her husband.

'You win, sir,' she muttered, and rose to leave. But a glint in the corner of the room caught her eye. She saw a small mirror there that she hadn't noticed before, and it was angled so that

Leofric could see her cards. She gave Leofric an accusatory glare, and he looked very guilty indeed.

'Bastard,' Godiva roared. Leofric went white. Godiva grabbed an iron poker from the fireplace and chased him round the table three times with it, but he was too fast and bolted out of the front door and down the street. Godiva chased him into the yard and, still wielding the poker, she jumped onto her horse and pursued Leofric through the middle of town.

It was market day, however, and the town was busy, so Leofric quickly escaped. Suddenly, Godiva realized that she was completely naked on a horse in Coventry town centre. All around her, men's mouths were hanging open and women were scowling and tutting at her. A painter who illuminated manuscripts for the local monastery whipped out his paints and began to illuminate a picture of the scene.

'Phwooar,' said the illuminator. 'Stick your chest out, love – that's it.' Before Godiva could react, he had painted a quick picture and was running as fast as he could to the monastery, shouting for the monk who edited the *Anglo-Saxon Chronicle*. Godiva could do little but ride to the nearest clothing stall and purchase a dress on credit before riding home in an absolute fury to drown her sorrows in a bottle of Pinot Grigio. Leofric was nowhere to be seen, for he was wisely laying low in the snug bar at the Viking's Fists.

Meanwhile, the illuminator was showing his painting to the abbot of the monastery, who was so struck by Godiva's beauty that he ordered the picture to run on page three of that week's *Anglo-Saxon Chronicle*, opposite a story about a Danish princess who had shown her knickers while getting onto a horse outside a London tavern. He paid the illuminator ten pieces of silver and the man trotted off to the pub, very happy with himself.

The next day, Godiva awoke with a vile headache to the sound of the *Anglo-Saxon Chronicle* sliding through her letterbox. When she opened it up and saw herself naked on her horse, she had the shock of her life.

'Glorious Godiva: I Love a Spot of Horseplay' read the article. 'High-born Lady Godiva, aged thirty-two, loves nothing more than to show off her 36-24-36 curves atop a fine stallion.'

Furious, Godiva snatched up the *Chronicle* and her iron poker from the fireplace and stormed down to the monastery, stamping past three illuminators who had set up camp in her driveway with their easels and paints. She got to the monastery and banged on the door for the abbot, and when he opened it, she chased him down the vaulted hallway.

'My lady,' he shrieked. 'I beg you – stop! How much do you want?'

'Eh?' said Godiva.

'For a six-month contract to appear on page three of the *Chronicle* every day,' panted the abbot. 'We sold out within two hours this morning. I've never seen anything like it. Everyone wants a copy. I've even heard that a bloke called Peeping Tom bought twenty copies! You're a hit – you could make a fortune! What do you say?'

'Hmm…' said Godiva.

Six months later, life was very different for Godiva. She no longer lived with the mean Leofric; she lived on her own in a smart city-centre wattle and daub penthouse with a bathtub and everything. She had a running contract with the *Anglo-Saxon Chronicle*, a franchised hand-illuminated calendar deal, an underwear range and her very own relationship advice column in a lads' parchment called *Wench*. She was very well off indeed but something nagged at her. The people of Coventry were still taxed too heavily, and she resolved to go and see Leofric about it one more time.

'Husband, I have proven myself an independent and worthy woman,' she said to him. 'Once more, I beg of you to lower the people's taxes.'

'Okay,' said Leofric.

'Really?' said Godiva.

'Yes,' said Leofric. 'You have done very well for yourself – and, as a consequence, you owe me a huge amount of tax. You owe me so much, in fact, that I can lower everyone else's taxes and still have even more funds for online poker than before. Your bill's in the post. Why are you smiling?'

'Because I've just thought of tomorrow's *Anglo-Saxon Chronicle* headline,' said Godiva, as she reached into the fireplace. 'It's going to say Leofric Leathered by Luscious Lady G.'

'Oh dear,' said Leofric, as the iron poker whistled through the air.

THE BATTLE OF HASTINGS: A BANK HOLIDAY RUINED

THE YEAR 1066 SAW TERRIBLE PROBLEMS WITH hooliganism in England, the worst incident of all being the Battle of Hastings. What began with a harmless online debate about who was hardest – England or Normandy – quickly spiralled out of control and ended with a bloody battle on Hastings' seafront that saw a royal dynasty overthrown, a country subjugated, and a Bank Holiday Monday ruined for thousands of day-trippers.

The summer had already seen a terrible hooligan riot between the English, led by King Harold, and a rampaging mob of Norwegians at Stamford Bridge. The English were victorious and several hooligans immediately went online to boast about how they'd walloped the invaders. Things became heated when Normandy fans based in France began to question the fitness of the Norwegian team, which led to mounting bad language between the English and the Normans, and culminated with King Harold calling William the Conqueror, Duke of Normandy, a sneaky nonce and a usurper. It was too late to back down now and the two leaders arranged to meet in the seaside resort of Hastings to sort it out with violence.

It was a hot bank holiday weekend and King Harold turned up at Hastings in a foul mood and with a raging thirst on. The English had already been drinking on the way down and they quickly began menacing families in the local inns, racing horses up and down the seafront and throwing fish and chips at each other. Several of them dropped their pants in public; others ran around with traffic cones on their heads and the town's respectable citizens tutted sternly at their antics.

With a great roar, the Normans ambushed the English from one end of the beach. Harold downed a final shot of tequila in the Viking's Head and summoned his guard of 'headhunters' – an elite regiment with tattooed hands and forearms, who had sworn never to run away or inform on each other to the authorities. As battle raged outside, they barricaded themselves inside the inn and held the doors against the invaders.

The Normans threw themselves against the pub doors for much of the day but were soundly beaten back by the English left outside the pub. Fists flew, noses squelched and fallen warriors were kicked between the legs. Suddenly Harold emerged from the inn and cracked William the Conqueror hard with a perfectly-executed headbutt to the forehead. William staggered, stumbled and crashed head-first into a litter bin and a great groan went up from the Norman side.

With their leader down, they retreated towards the pier. Drunk and excited, the headhunters piled out of the pub to join the rest of the English and chased their enemies onto the beach, tipping over a whelk stand, hurling ice cream everywhere and terrifying innocent holidaymakers.

However, William was not completely out for the count. That morning, he had carefully put on several chequered baseball caps, one underneath the other, which had cushioned the blow. Now he removed his headgear and shinned up a lamppost, rallying his troops back into the fight and bellowing at great volume as several English hooligans tugged vainly at his legs. The Normans surged forward with renewed vigour and, in the middle of the new fray, William the Conqueror cracked Harold hard in the face with a heavy glass ashtray from a pub table.

'AAAAAGH,' Harold howled. 'STOP THE FIGHT – IT HURTS!'

'Bloody hell,' said one of the English soldiers. 'It was supposed to be no weapons.'

Harold's eye was literally hanging out. An Englishman fainted. Two Normans threw up on the spot. The elite headhunters stopped what they were doing and trotted back into the pub to find a first-aid kit.

'AAAAAGH,' cried Harold. 'Get me to casualty!'

'Seriously, I think we should,' said a Norman knight.

'Why are you all bloody looking at me?' said William the Conqueror. 'All right – fine, I'll take him.'

William threw the wailing Harold over the back of his horse and galloped at speed to the local hospital. The English and Normans looked at each other sheepishly. The air was thick with dust, they all stank of beer and everyone felt slightly embarrassed.

'My wife's probably expecting me home,' said one of the headhunters quietly.

'Yeah…' said a Norman. 'Better go and pick the kids up from archery practice.'

As King Harold staggered into casualty, defeated and clutching his eye socket, both sides slunk away into the night. Although he had technically cheated, William the Conqueror took the throne the next day, after King Harold said he was done with fighting. And, although the Normans would settle here and eventually become English themselves, the English have had a slight distrust of the French ever since.

THE DOMESDAY WEEKEND

EUSTACE OF SUSSEX HOLDS THREE HIDES IN THE MANOR *of Dallington, some horses, many pigs and a Sega MasterSystemme with three games. He is to provide the king with six knights and twelve men at arms under the wartime levy. He doth tithe to the church three shillings per annum and oweth sixpence to Martin the Dealer. He lists his ethnicity as White British and his religion as Jedi, though I suspect this to be a prank.*

THE DOMESDAY BOOK

Having won the Battle of Hastings, William the Conqueror had a new problem. He had fallen in love with the beautiful Matilda of Flanders only to discover she was an old-fashioned type who believed in getting married before engaging in night-time activity. William had duly proposed to her and they were to be married in the summer – but first, there was the matter of the stag weekend.

William could have held it in Normandy, where he came from, but this didn't seem right – after all, he reasoned, he should be going out on the lash somewhere in newly conquered England. However, he had no idea where to go for the best pubs, plunder, strippers and paintballing. William didn't want a simple night out on the town – he wanted the biggest and best stag do in history. Nothing short of utter carnage would do – this weekend had to resemble Domesday.

William had just attended his friend Odo of Bayeux's stag weekend, and he knew it would be a tough act to follow. The raucous trip had seen a raiding party of a hundred Norman knights descend upon the town of Exeter, where they had got disgustingly drunk for three days, had gone paintballing, plundered herds of pigs and cows and roasted them, visited several lapdancing clubs and burned the entire town while laughing hysterically. Finally the party had ridden back to London with several captive women.

After that, William knew that he had to pull something special out of the bag – and first he needed to find out where the best pubs, strippers and inflammable thatched houses in his kingdom were. Suddenly, he had a flash of inspiration. He would send a taskforce of people up and down the country with a big book, recording what was in every town and village. That way he could research where to hold the stag weekend to beat all stag weekends. He summoned his clerks at once, told them his plan and sent them out with a huge, empty book and some clipboards; then he skipped over to Matilda's house and explained that the wedding would need to be postponed for a week or two.

However, after a month, William's clerks had only managed to survey a few counties in the south-east. Matilda suggested that Brighton might be a nice spot for a weekend of plunder and pillage but William was having none of it, for he was worried that someone else might find a better destination later. He told Matilda that he would hold fast and arrange nothing until his book was complete. Then he gently enquired whether she might consider bending her marriage-first rule just once, given that they were properly engaged and everything. Matilda glared at William in a manner that made him feel really quite uncomfortable, and he decided not to mention it again.

Two weeks later, William's pal, Walter of Calais, announced his engagement and that he was holding his stag weekend in Worcester. The knights drank every inn dry, downed flaming tequila shots, put every male adult to the sword, burned a monastery with all the monks in it and, finally, went paintballing. As a special prank, William had Walter blinded with a red-hot poker and bound to a lamppost with an L-sign on his pants. Everyone agreed that Walter's was quite the best stag do ever.

'Not for long,' thought William. 'Not for long.'

A month later, William summoned his clerks and demanded his book. Trembling, they informed him that it was still not finished: they had only managed to cover the southern half of England, which meant that the north was still a mystery. William couldn't take it any more. He grabbed the book from them and summoned his army. He would finish the rest of it himself and then have his stag weekend.

William and his knights rode north, until they found the village his clerks had not inventoried and got started. It didn't go well. All of the villagers ran away and the chickens kept moving when William tried to count them. After half an hour of trying to catalogue the village's wealth, he snapped. He grabbed a flaming torch, burned the whole place down and sat grumpily on a tree stump, smoking.

'At least we don't have to count the village now, sire,' said an aide. 'We can get the book finished more quickly.'

'That's not a bad idea,' thought William. If they burned the whole of the north, they could get the book finished in no time as there would be nothing left to count. Better still, they could make this pillage of the north the actual stag weekend and William could finally get married and enjoy the affections of the beautiful Matilda. He gathered his generals, told them the plan and sent word to London to prepare for his wedding on Monday. A great cheer went up and a comedy pair of plastic breasts was affixed to William's head. The stag weekend was on.

The weekend is remembered as the Harrying of the North.

William and his knights went on the rampage, burning every single thing they could find. They raced horses and carts around barns and then set them on fire; they put the male population to the sword; they hired strippers in their hundreds; they ran up vast bar bills and then torched the pubs – and they even got to go paintballing. Everyone said that it was a stag weekend fit for a conqueror and would never be matched.

William woke up in London on the morning of his wedding with an appalling hangover. He opened his book, jotted down that the north of England was just a few burnt settlements and slammed it shut. The book was finished – and his stag weekend had indeed resembled Domesday.

The wedding went without a hitch. Odo of Bayeux remembered the rings and gave a hilariously risqué speech about the events of the weekend and how he would have married Matilda had he seen her first. The day passed like a blur and soon enough the couple were at a lovely hotel where William began to disrobe. Finally, he would enjoy the charms of Matilda of Flanders. But Matilda recoiled in horror.

William the Conqueror looked down at his bare chest. There, scrawled in marker pen, were the words 'Tallulah the Fair, Newcastle's Number One Lapdancer Woz 'ere'.

William spent his wedding night on the floor.

RICHARD THE
LIONHEART GOES
ON A CRUSADE

I N 1095, POPE URBAN II HELD A GREAT MEETING IN THE
French town of Clermont to call on every king, knight and
commoner in Europe to go and fight in the Holy Land and the
Mediterranean – and the greatest of all the kings who answered
the call was Richard I of England, otherwise known as Richard
the Lionheart.

Richard the Lionheart was strong in spirit and body; a
warrior and a gentleman. On hearing of the Pope's crusade, he
went home at once to raise a great army of knights, men-at-
arms and archers. He packed a bag with sunscreen, shades and
his armour, mounted his horse and rode through Europe at the
head of his great army, meeting up with other Crusader armies

in Italy from where they all embarked for the Holy Land together. After a long sea voyage, Richard and the Crusaders made landfall at Antioch in modern-day Turkey, where they disembarked, fell to their knees and kissed the sand.

After they had knelt there kissing the sand for a while, Richard rose to his feet.

'Who's in charge then?' he said.

'I thought you were in charge,' said a French duke named Godfrey de Bouillon.

'Fine – I am here to fight,' said Richard, puffing his chest out.

'Me too,' said Godfrey, clapping his hand to the hilt of his great sword. 'Who are we fighting again?'

'Bugger,' said Richard. 'I left before the Pope got onto that bit. Does anybody know who we're fighting?'

There was a resounding silence as thousands of knights shifted nervously and scratched their helmets. It seemed that no one had been paying attention at the Pope's meeting.

'Well,' said an archer, 'shall we go and get a drink while we try to remember?'

'It's very hot out here,' said Godfrey. 'I could use a pint and there's a bar over there.'

'TO THE BAR!' roared Richard the Lionheart. Trumpets

were sounded, a great cheer went up and the Crusader army advanced up the beach to an outdoor bar named 'Sultan Dreamz'. They swarmed in, singing raucous songs and laughing at things on the menu that sounded like English swear words. They stayed there all afternoon and were entertained in the evening by an enterprising local who read out pirated copies of the latest chivalric ballads from back home.

After the bar closed, though, the Crusaders wanted more fun, and they took to the streets of Antioch. There, they stumbled across a tour rep who offered them a thirty-groat all-you-can-drink bar crawl up and down the main strip. Many shots were drunk and the Crusaders, who were suffering the effects of the Mediterranean sun, began to get rowdy. At Hattin's English Pub, a fist-fight erupted and when the Byzantine emperor John Comnenus tried to intervene, he was glassed by a longbowman from Slough. Comnenus staggered outside to declare war on his Crusader allies only to find that his horse had been stolen and ridden into the sea.

On the main strip, Crusaders had begun drunkenly racing up and down the road on rented ponies and two groups of knights from London began stabbing each other after Sir Walter of E7 disrespected Sir Ranulph of SW9. Meanwhile, a nobleman named Stephen of Blois tumbled off a nightclub balcony, fracturing his collarbone and losing several teeth.

As chaos erupted up and down the strip, Richard the Lionheart and Godfrey were arguing with two nightclub bouncers who were refusing their party entry to the city's premier venue – Palmz Nite Club – on account of the Crusaders having removed their armour from the waist up. An almighty row soon kicked off and several knights took advantage of the distraction to sneak into the nightclub through the fire escape and open the doors, allowing Richard's personal bodyguard to lead an assault on the bar. Local clubbers fled the building as a raucous round of flaming tequila shots started a fire that engulfed the bar and quickly spread to the neighbouring buildings. Suddenly, the local police arrived on the scene, panicking and angry, with truncheons held aloft.

'*That's* who we're supposed to be fighting,' roared Richard the Lionheart, and he swung a great punch with his mailed fist that knocked a policeman flat as more Crusaders and more police piled in.

By the time the sun came up, the ancient city of Antioch had been pillaged and burned to the ground. Thousands of locals and Crusaders lay dead and the remnants of the Crusader army were sobering up in the local police station.

To a man, the Crusaders were sunburned, hungover and very dejected – all except one, that is.

'That was brilliant,' croaked Richard the Lionheart. 'Shall we all come again next year?'

'YOU WILL NOT COME AGAIN,' yelled the police sergeant. 'YOU ARE ALL DEPORTED AND BANNED!'

'Let's go to Faliraki instead,' said Godfrey de Bouillon.

BAD KING JOHN'S BAD FEEDBACK

KING JOHN, WHO WOULD SIGN THE GREAT DOCUMENT called the Magna Charta, which is the basis of English law, came to the throne with serious financial troubles. John was the younger brother of Richard the Lionheart, who spent England's money on crusading. By the time Richard died of an arrow wound sustained during a bar fight in Malia, leaving the throne to John, the country was completely broke.

John didn't even have enough money for a proper crown, and he would spend all day pacing up and down his castle, wondering how he could get his hands on some loot. England was already taxed to the hilt. There was always conquering and pillaging but John's armour was broken and he could barely feed his horses. One day, however, as he looked from the window at the mangy animals, an idea slowly formed in his mind, and he called for every citizen of London to come to the Tower at once.

When they arrived, John was nowhere to be seen. Instead, they found a few words written on the castle door: 'Horse for sale. Reasonable condition. Write bids on parchment. Auction starts at one groat. Ends tonight. Vendor: SmoothKing1165.' Below the writing was a drawing of King John's horse.

'Not bad,' said a shoemaker. 'I'll pay two groats for it.'

'Hang on,' said a baker. 'I'm bidding two and a half.'

'I'll wait until the very end and bid when it's almost finished,' said a merchant, who was sneaky like that, but no one paid any attention to him and they all began frantically writing their own bids on the door.

Shortly afterwards, the baker remembered that he had some flour he needed to get rid of, so he drew a picture of it on the door and wrote a little note to go with it. Soon, everyone was posting items for sale on the castle door and bidding for other people's things and writing feedback about the people they'd done business with, and there was quite a clamour.

The next day, King John wandered downstairs where he found his chancellor waiting for him with a bag of gold. His horse had sold for eighty groats. Quick as a flash, he scuttled upstairs to see what else he could find to sell. His eyes settled on his old suit of armour that he never wore because it was missing several rivets and was liable to fall apart in battle.

John quickly ran down to the castle door, drew a picture of the armour and wrote:

'Suit of armour: men's, size large. Needs repairs. Vendor: SmoothKing1165.'

Then, he looked around him and saw how many people were gathered and how much money was changing hands.

'Hmmm…' he thought, and crossed out 'Needs repairs' and replaced it with 'Mint condition'. People started bidding on the armour straight away, particularly the Earl of Gloucester who had outgrown his own suit and needed a replacement. Meanwhile, more people showed up to buy and sell things on the door. John bolted indoors and started fishing everything out of the royal cupboards, broken or not. He found some old robes, a sundial, a few pots and pans, a gold cup or two and a crown that didn't fit – and he advertised it all on the door.

A few days later John sprinted downstairs to find out how rich he was – but he was in for a shock. Apart from the armour, none of his items had sold and on the door was scrawled:

'Bad feedback for seller SmoothKing1165. Sold me faulty suit of armour (helmet fell apart while fighting Scots). Now missing an ear. Avoid.' The note was signed EarlofPimp89.

John flew into a wild rage, feverishly scratched out the note and had the Earl of Gloucester thrown into a dungeon. After this, he bid for several other items, won the auctions and ordered his guards to remove the goods without paying. When the sellers posted their own bad feedback about him, he had them thrown into the dungeons as well. This worked so well for King John that he repeated it the next day and then again the day after that.

It was a year of great hardship, the chronicler Gerald of Wales wrote later. *No man did any work for all were trying to buy and sell things on the door of the Tower. Every man lived in fear of the king, who abused the system at will. When men wised up to his username, he changed it; any man that complained was thrown into the dungeons. I myself got drunk one night and purchased a set of cart wheels from the bastard. They didn't even match.*

Meanwhile, John sat in the Tower counting his loot and laughing to himself. He was a rich man thanks to his auction rip-offs. He had several suits of armour, a whole yard full of new horses and lots and lots of money. Outside, the auction frenzy continued unabated although many users were either broke or in the dungeon. One day, however, the din outside went quiet and John popped out for a look. What he saw made his blood run cold. The door was gone and so were all the people. In their place was a single note, which read:

'One castle door. Excellent condition. Lots of writing on one side. Buyer collects from field by River Thames in Runnymede. Must collect today or door will be burned. Seller: DisgruntledBarons32.'

King John was terrified. The door was his livelihood. He saddled up his fastest new horse and galloped down to Runnymede to bid for his door back. When he arrived, he found several armed barons waiting for him, who seized him, sat him down and presented him with a huge document and a quill pen.

'Sign,' said one of the barons, 'or the door gets it. Look over there.'

The door was sitting on top of a giant bonfire and another baron stood there with a burning torch, ready to light it. The quill pen was thrust into John's trembling hand.

'I haven't read what I'm bloody signing,' wailed the panicking king.

'It's fine,' said the baron. 'Just the ownership deeds to the door and some small print called the Magna Charta. It forbids you from imprisoning people who write bad feedback about you and obliges you to settle auction debts properly. There are a few other legal bits as well. Ooh look – that torch is getting pretty close to the bonfire.'

'Fine!' yelled King John. 'I'll sign – just let me have the door back.'

The next day, John sulkily let everyone who had written bad feedback about him out of the dungeon and, ever since then, kings and queens have had to respect the civil rights laid out in the Magna Charta – as well as paying vendors properly for items purchased at auction.

ROBIN THE HOODIE OUTWITS THE SHERIFF

ROBIN THE HOODIE, THAT MOST FAMOUS AND ROMANTIC of British rogues, lived near Nottingham in the time of King John. As a young man, Robin was outlawed for breaking into the king's carriage and stealing gold and a pair of sunglasses from the glove compartment. An elderly woman spotted him fleeing the scene and described him to the king's guards as a 'robbing hoodie type'. The name stuck.

Robin fled to the safety of his local park in Nottingham, where he decided that he would steal gold, silver and iPods from rich joggers and dog-walkers to give to the poor. He soon attracted a gang of vagabonds and outlaws who lived in the park with him. There was Litter John, a large youth who left a trail of fried chicken wrappers, cigarette butts and crisp packets wherever he went, there was the wily Will Scarface, and there was Much the Dealer's son, who was famed for the quality of his Lincoln Green. They were also joined by a rogue chip shop worker named Friar Tuck who could always be relied upon to crack heads should an enemy call him Triar Fuck.

Robin and his gang were famous for their skill at spitting, and Robin himself was the greatest of all. It was said that he could place a wad of phlegm between a flying pigeon's eyes at two hundred feet – and it was by this skill that his enemy, the Sheriff of Nottingham, would try to bring about his downfall.

The Sheriff was responsible for preventing antisocial behaviour in the Nottingham area and Robin the Hoodie was a constant thorn in his side. Every time the Sheriff went to the park, Robin would hit him on the back of the neck with a wad of spit and, one time, the outlaw smeared dog excrement under the door handle of the Sheriff's carriage. The Sheriff tried and tried to think of ways to catch Robin but the youth was too nimble. Then one day he had an idea.

The sheriff sent for a tailor and had the man make a beautiful, silver-coloured hooded sweatshirt with diamante zips and gold-embroidered dollar signs all over it. Then, he announced that he would be holding a city-wide spitting competition and that the beautiful silver hoodie would be the prize. He knew that Robin would never be able to resist the challenge and he knew that when Robin turned up, his men-at-arms could pounce on the troublesome youth.

Back in the park, Robin and his gang were busy vandalizing the swings when word of the competition reached them. At once they stopped, lit a joint of Lincoln Green and began debating what to do.

'It is a trick of the Sheriff's,' cried Litter John. 'We must not go.'

'Perhaps you weren't listening,' said Robin. 'It is a silver hoodie with diamante zips and gold-embroidery dollar signs on it. I *must* have it.'

'We could disguise ourselves,' said Friar Tuck. 'Let's mug some weedy Goth kids and steal their clothes.'

'Like it,' said Robin. 'Gang – let's go.'

The outlaws crept up behind a group of weedy Goth youths who were sitting under a tree writing poetry and complaining about their parents. Quick as a flash, they covered the Goths in spit, tied them up, dressed themselves in the Goths' clothes, put on a spot of eyeliner, dyed their hair purplish-black and set off for the spitting contest in town.

The competition was to be held underneath the walls of

Nottingham castle and a great many people had turned out to watch. The Sheriff had drawn a red line on the ground, behind which the competitors had to stand. Their target – a row of empty cola cans – was fifty yards away. Robin and his gang lined up with the other contestants and hawked up their best phlegm in preparation.

A trumpet sounded and the competition began. A hundred youths began spitting at the row of cola cans as all of the townspeople watched, applauding whenever someone landed a direct hit. Robin and his gang shot splendidly. Each one of them hit his can with every single phlegm wad, and Robin was getting most of his inside the 'o' of the cola logo.

Above them, the Sheriff was pacing the walls of his castle looking for the outlaws but he could see no sign of them – just a bunch of youths and a few Goth kids. Where were the outlaws? Surely they were on their way and would arrive soon.

As the competition went on, those who missed their cans began to be eliminated. Fresh cans were brought out and placed progressively further and further away until only two contestants were left: Robin and an out-of-town champion named Darren of Doncaster who spat through his two front teeth with deadly accuracy.

A final can was brought out and placed a full hundred yards away and Darren of Doncaster stepped up to the mark first. He squinted, tossed a few blades of grass in the air to test the wind direction, and then spat. His yellowed mass of mucus whistled through the air and struck the can with a plink. The crowd murmured its approval and waited to see what the unknown Goth would do. Robin stepped up, hawked up a vast lump of phlegm and blew it as hard as he could. The phlegm soared long and high and then plopped right into the open spout of the can. The crowd went wild.

Robin stepped onto a podium to collect his prize from the Sheriff himself, who had still not recognized the young outlaw underneath his eyeliner and baggy black clothes. Beaming with pride, Robin slipped on the silver hoodie and bowed left and right. As he did so, however, the hood popped over his head. The Sheriff gasped as he recognized his enemy and his hand went for his sword. Robin reacted quickly, spitting into the Sheriff's open mouth and springing off the podium into the crowd as the Sheriff gagged and choked.

The outlaws found each other among the throng and fled, Litter John covering their retreat with a deadly hail of greasy kebab trays that caused the Sheriff's men to slip and slide everywhere. The Sheriff himself trod on a particularly greasy specimen and fell right onto his coccyx. As he ranted and raged on the floor and howled something about suing the council for this, the outlaws fled back to the park, where they melted into the woods to spend the evening drinking cider, smoking Lincoln Green and admiring Robin's new silver hoodie.

GEORGE CHASES
THE DRAGON

WHEN THE CRUSADERS RETURNED FROM THEIR TRIPS abroad, they brought back many new things: spices, silks, precious stones, new foods and, above all, they returned with remarkable stories. The greatest story of all was the tale of George and the Dragon, a tale that would eventually become England's national myth.

George was a brave and flawless knight who travelled from city to city doing good deeds. One day, he rode into a town where all the people were weeping. When he asked them what the matter was, they told him that their lives were being made a misery by a great dragon with a terrible drugs habit. To appease the dragon, they had to give it all their pocket change every time they walked past it, which made them very poor and miserable because the change was all they had.

That day, it happened that it was the turn of the king's daughter to give the dragon all of her change. She was a pretty girl and the occasion was a particularly woeful one because she had just had a birthday and was flush with money her relations had given her. It did not matter that she was the king's daughter, for everyone without exception had to draw lots to decide who would walk past the drug-addicted dragon and be menaced into turning out their pockets.

69

George could not abide this and he vowed on his shining sword that he would accompany her and defeat the terrible dragon. He lifted the princess onto the back of his horse and the pair set off to the corner of town where the dragon lurked outside the bus station.

The smell of acrid smoke grew stronger and stronger as they neared the spot, and when they rounded the corner, George saw it. The huge dragon lay on the ground, its great snout buried in a sheet of tin foil on which its drugs smouldered. It wore a reeking leather jacket and striped tracksuit bottoms; its face was pale and scarred and it seemed to have lost its shoelaces. George lowered his lance and rode towards it with the king's daughter whimpering into his shoulder.

The dragon saw them and leapt up in all its ruined splendour to block the pavement. George swerved right and then left but the dragon was too fast and mirrored his moves exactly. It towered over George and told him, in a voice thick with hisses and crackles, that it had eaten nothing for three days and needed his change for a sandwich.

'I will purchase you a sandwich,' George said. 'Accompany me to the sandwich shop.'

'No,' hissed the dragon. 'I cannot, for I was mugged around the corner from here and they stole my shoes, so I cannot walk.

Give me change for new shoes.'

'You have shoes on your feet,' said George, who was quick-witted and sharp.

'But I am saving these shoes for my long walk home,' hissed the dragon. 'I lost my bus ticket and must now walk all the way. Give me your change for a bus ticket.'

'You want money for smack,' roared George. 'Have at you!'

With this, he drew his sword and lunged for the dragon. It ducked the blow, pulled a craft knife from its leather jacket and waved it hypnotically. The two adversaries circled each other, neither making a move.

'Want some drugs?' said the dragon.

'What?' said George.

'Have some drugs,' said the dragon. 'They'll keep you sleek and trim. You could stand to lose a couple of pounds.'

'Bastard,' cried George, and lunged once again at the dragon, because he was sensitive about his weight. Faster than lightning, the dragon parried with its craft knife, whipped out its bag of drugs and belched a great flame over them which shrouded George in noxious smoke.

'You fucker,' said George as he fell over and passed out.

George came around much later in the day to find the dragon sitting counting the princess's birthday money, which it had demanded from her as soon as George hit the deck.

'Ooh,' said George. 'I feel rather trembly. Have you got any more? Just to take the edge off, like.'

'Are you kidding?' said the dragon. 'First one is free. Subsequent hits will cost you.'

'But I haven't got any money,' George complained.

'Oh *dear*,' hissed the dragon sarcastically. George's blood boiled. He could take no more of the beast, and he drew his sword and advanced.

'Hold on,' said the dragon. 'I'm the only one around here who knows where to get the stuff.'

An hour later, the townspeople saw a horse approaching with a figure slumped in the saddle. It was George. They lifted him down from his mount and brought him water to drink. After a while, he lifted his head weakly.

'I have slain the beast,' George croaked, and all the townspeople gave a great cheer. They laid on a magnificent feast for him and, after he was fed, they brought him a fresh horse and presented him with a big bag of gold. That evening, George rode away into the sunset and the townspeople wished him well and thanked him and applauded him until he was long out of sight.

'That's funny,' said one of the townspeople after a while.

'He wasn't supposed to be heading in that direction.'

'No,' said another. 'He went the way the dragon used to be before he bravely slew it.'

'Oh bugger,' said a third townsperson.

A few hours later, George turned up again. He looked pale and spotty, and the chainmail lace was missing from one of his armoured shoes.

'Can I have some change, please?' begged George.

'What happened to your bag of gold?' demanded the townspeople.

'I needed it for something,' George replied, drawing his sword. 'Now give me some change.'

'Bloody hell,' said the townspeople, and handed over their change.

George trudged back to the corner by the bus station where the dragon lived and handed half the money to it. The pair got royally wasted and then set about menacing passers-by for more change. George is said to dwell by the bus station still, and legend has it that if the realm of England is ever in trouble, its citizens only need to jingle the change in their pockets and George will appear at the very head of the English army, where he will terrify our enemies by ordering them to lend him a tenner to get the train home.

Edward II: A Royal Eye for the Straight Knight

KING EDWARD I WAS A GREAT AND MIGHTY KING, WHO loved to fight and drink. A man's man, he was known as the Hammerer of the Scotch for the amount of booze he could put away – and he would still be ready for a battle first thing in the morning. The only thing that really troubled him was his son, the future Edward II.

This strange youth didn't seem at all warlike like his father and, as for booze, it was rumoured that the only thing he would touch was gin. His favourite companion was a flamboyant young knight named Piers Gaveston; together, the pair would spend their time giggling, whispering and criticizing the facial hair of the king's favourite knights. When the gruff Edward found out that his son had been skipping his jousting lessons to hang around in the woods reading French poetry, he realized that something had to be done.

Edward I sat his son down and explained that his behaviour was most unkingly – that England needed a rough warrior ruler – but young Edward refused to listen and flounced petulantly off to his chamber, where he locked the door and refused to come out. For several days, the king waited patiently, even pushing plates of food under the door, but, eventually, he lost his temper and broke it down. A rope was dangling from the window and his son was nowhere to be seen.

In a fit of panic, the king ordered that the kingdom be scoured for his whereabouts. It was a full three days before news came back. The prince had been discovered disgustingly drunk in a tavern in the village of Vauxhall, surrounded by sailors and listening to minstrels from the continent. The king went very red and called for his sword. Then he clutched his left arm and collapsed.

Edward II's coronation was an uneasy one. England was in trouble: the Scots were massed on the border and the Welsh were ready to revolt. Nonetheless, Edward II stood up and vowed to give the country the leadership it needed. He announced that he would form a council of five leaders to govern the kingdom and that all the barons were to report to the Tower that very evening to receive further instructions from him.

When the barons arrived, they found that Edward had been busy. The rushes that normally carpeted the floor of the great hall had been removed and replaced by a great beige carpet. The stone walls of the hall had been tastefully decorated with tapestries from Italy and the torches that lit the room had been replaced with soft candles.

'What wrongness is this?' roared the burly Earl of Arundel.

'I quite like it actually,' said the Earl of Pembroke. 'Very minimalist.'

'Seize the Earl of Arundel,' Edward shouted, leaping out from behind a silk drape. 'There are going to be some changes around here.'

Quick as a flash, Piers Gaveston and four handsome clean-cut knights charged out from the four corners of the room, grabbed the Earl of Arundel and bundled him outside screaming. The other barons watched in fearful silence. Certain that Arundel was to die the traitor's death of hanging, drawing and quartering, they said not a word.

The earl was dragged through the streets of London to a merchant's house, where he was bound and tied tightly to a firm chair. One of the knights drew out a wicked-looking blade and held it to the earl's throat. Arundel closed his eyes and prepared for death. But death did not come. Instead, a band of minstrels somewhere in the room struck up a cheery and catchy tune. Arundel opened his eyes and realized that the handsome knight was actually shaving off his great bushy beard. Alarmed, he looked around to see the king staring at him with a look of great concentration.

'Style em-ERGENCY!' cried Edward. 'Go, go, go, Fab Knights!'

The earl struggled and strained but it was no good. The knights shaved him clean, cut his hair into a fetching cut that framed his face, and went about his eyebrows with a pair of tweezers. Next, the earl's armour was stripped off and he was plunged into a hot bath, pulled out, roughly dried off and dressed in a contemporary tunic with gold embroidery and a pair of Italian leather boots.

The knights bundled him onto a horse and galloped him to the palace kitchens, where one Fab Knight showed him how to prepare a sushi dinner and talked him through the finer points of comtemporary music. Finally, he was ridden back home to his castle, where Edward and another of his Fab Knights redecorated his banqueting hall.

The next day, the barons were astonished to see the Earl of Arundel walk into the great hall of the Tower of London, not only alive but smelling nice, looking clean and walking with a distinct spring in his step.

'Well?' said Edward.

'Well…' replied the earl slowly, 'Mrs Arundel was impressed.'

'How impressed?' said Edward.

'Like… FOUR TIMES impressed,' the earl roared. The barons looked at each other in silence for a moment and then the chamber descended into uproar.

Edward and his Fab Knights found themselves very busy indeed that year, the chronicler Adam Murimuth wrote. *Despite a few early reservations, every baron and knight in the kingdom eventually lined up for their services. Castles were redecorated in bright and tasteful themes. French wine was not only drunk but discussed over dinner. The medicinal spa at Bath did a roaring trade, as did tailors, haircutters and fingernail buffers. At the centre of it all, Edward II was celebrated far and wide as the leading light of a new golden age. It could have lasted forever were it not for the revolutionary new beauty treatment which arrived from France in 1327. With the benefit of hindsight, red-hot poker colonic irrigation was obviously a step too far.*

THE BLACK PRINCE: ENGLAND'S PREMIER KNIGHT

HE BLACK PRINCE, THE MOST FAMOUS OF ALL THE knights of England, won his spurs during the dark days of the Hundred Years War with France, a time when every young man in the kingdom dreamed of proving himself on the field of battle.

One of the most significant battles of the war was the Battle of Crécy, where just fifteen thousand English troops found themselves up against fifty thousand Frenchmen. The prince's father, King Edward III, considered him too young for his first team of knights and the prince was forced to wait in reserve as the battle went badly for his side. Hopelessly outnumbered, the English found themselves on the back foot straight away and, by the time eighty-nine minutes of battle had passed, defeat seemed assured.

'Father,' cried the prince, 'let me fight! I promise to give it a hundred and ten per cent on the field. Literally!'

The king, who was very red in the face from shouting at his knights from the sidelines, looked at his son and nodded. Many of the older knights laughed and scoffed as the prince rode onto the field but the lad simply fixed them with a steely look and lowered his lance.

Suddenly, the most fearsome warrior in France, the burly, dirty-fighting Count of Zidane, singled the Black Prince out and charged. The battlefield fell silent and every man held his breath. At the last second, the prince neatly side-stepped the count and a great cheer went up from the English side. The prince galloped down the field, swerving two French dukes and leaping a third, throwing the defence into confusion. As he approached the French king he feinted left, then right, then smashed him so hard with his sword that his severed head flew fifty yards into the French camp. A deafening roar went up on the English side. The battle was won. The English knights carried the prince from the field in glory, pausing occasionally to swap helmets with the French knights – and a hero was born.

The English can not get enough of their new star, wrote the chronicler Geoffrey of Monmouth a year later. *The lance-makers AdiLance hath given him a sponsorship deal worth many hundreds of groats, as hath the helmet-maker Helmbro. We hope that his reported romance with the Lady Joan doth not distract him from his duty at the forthcoming Calais fixture next year.*

The lady in question was a beautiful noblewoman known as the Fair Wag of Kent. Famous for her love of well-paid knights, she had made a beeline for the young prince at the West London ball in 1346 and the pair had become a fixture on the front page of every tabloid manuscript. No party or theatre opening night was complete without them and, when Edward III announced that his son was promoted to captain of the English army, the Black Prince became the foremost figure in the land. As he won battle after battle, everyone – including he – came to believe that he was invincible.

In 1347, the whole country turned out to watch the prince's next big fixture: the siege of Calais. The walled French town was renowned for its strong defences, and taverns all over England rang with arguments about what formation the English army should take. The battle proved to be a tough one. The English knights struggled to breach the walls despite giving it their all, and several were literally gutted. Then, the

French champion challenged the prince to a duel. It was a well-fought battle and both warriors hacked and parried in front of the walls for a long time, until suddenly the Black Prince hoofed the Frenchman in the groin – a clear foul. A red banner was unfurled and the prince was ordered off the field.

Luckily, starvation forced the citizens of Calais to surrender and disaster was averted, but the prince's reputation was tarnished. Although the country still loved him, he moved to Spain to fight for the King of Madrid, where he won a resounding victory with a second-half kill from the halfway line at the Battle of Nájera. Later, he distinguished himself in an international fixture at Limoges in Aquitaine, massacring three thousand of the town's inhabitants.

By the time he was thirty, the prince was earning as much money from sponsorship as he was making from his ordinary looting and plunder on the battlefield. The Royal Armoury paid him a substantial sum to endorse their flagship range of armour and he also signed a five-year deal to promote a new cloth from the east known as cotton – a very forward fashion statement. The prince also endorsed a range of crowns, thrones, medicinal leeches, daggers, spurs, loincloths and a luxury range of turnips, as well as launching the popular BlackPrince line of perfumes with his wife.

But then disaster struck:

It grieves me to report, wrote the chronicler Froissart, *that terrible news is arrived from Spain. The Black Prince hath disappeared across the sea after signing a ten-thousand-groat deal to fight in a place known as America. I know… I know. The place hath not even been officially discovered yet, but 'tis rumoured to be very glamorous. The prince hath announced that he journeys there to promote our own form of warfare in that distant land, for they do fight differently and hath not even heard of the offside rule. Like all good Englishmen, I blame the Fair Wag of Kent for this mischief and wish the Prince all speed in retrieving his balls from her handbag and coming swiftly back.*

Tragically, the earth was still flat in those days and the Black Prince and his wife are believed to have fallen off the edge.

THE PEASANTS' REVOLT AND THE BIRTH OF SOCIAL NETWORKING

I N 1381, LIFE WAS DIFFICULT IN THE COUNTRYSIDE. A TERRIBLE plague called the Black Death had wiped out a third of the labour force. Peasants were beginning to clamour for better working conditions. Now, the Hundred Years War with France had become so expensive that a new tax was needed to pay for it. This tax was called the Poll Tax, and it charged households according to how many people were in each family. In an age before proper birth control or confectionery wrappers, this was a terrible burden.

One day, in the Essex village of Fobbing, a strange thing occurred. A scrap of paper with 'I bet I can find a hundred people AGAINST the Pole tax' written on it was found pinned to a tree. A crowd of people gathered around the tree and, although no one knew who had written the note, several people added their signatures to it.

The next day, the villagers found a new note pinned to the tree, which read: 'There ripping us off, Lets Get ten thouzand members against the Pole Tax.' As news spread of the tree, people began to come from miles around to add their signature, and, by the end of the day, the note had six hundred names underneath it. Several comments had also been added. One, by a man named Wat Tyler, read: 'Let's March on London and tell those basterds LOL!' There was also one which read 'I preferred the old note: BRING BACK OLD NOTE who agree's with me?' which several villagers put their signatures to as well.

The following week, the rumblings of discontent were beginning to spread. A note by a priest named John Ball pinned to a tree in nearby Braintree read:

'I bet I can find fifty thousand people who think when Adam delved and Eve span, who THEN was the Gentleman? From the beginning all men by nature were created alike, and our bondage (LOL!!!) or servitude came in by the unjust oppression of wicked men.'

The note accumulated more than eight thousand signatures. Meanwhile, a note on a tree in Kent, which read 'If one hundred thousand people join this group the Peasants will march on London and behead the Archbishop of Canterbury' had attracted ninety-eight thousand signatures. Rumours began to spread of a Peasants' Revolt: a march on London to rid England of the hated Poll Tax, end the system of rural servitude and establish a new law to 'get sick fux who write jokes on trees about dead Black Death victims BANNED from writing things on trees'.

Word of the troubles in the countryside soon reached the king. Richard II was just fifteen, and he spent a great deal of his own time writing notes on trees. He ignored the peasants' concerns, though, preferring to read the notes written by the day's greatest entertainers and minstrels and write comments like 'FIT' on notes left by the young women of the palace. By the time the king's advisers made him pay attention to the problem, the Kent note had obtained its last two thousand signatures. An army of peasants was now marching on London with rusty scythes.

With Wat Tyler at their head, the peasants stormed across London Bridge, burned the tax records, broke open the Marshalsea prison, ransacked the Tower of London and dragged the Archbishop of Canterbury out of his palace and beheaded him. With London ablaze and in chaos, a note was found pinned to the palace door that read: 'If one King will meet us at Mile End to hear our demand's, we will tell him our demand's and stop burning the city.'

The king had little choice but to agree. The next day, he rode out with his men-at-arms to meet the peasant army at Mile End outside the city. There were tens of thousands of them, all angrily writing notes and pinning them up on any tree available. A chubby, tired-looking man named Wat Tyler approached from the multitude, carrying a pile of notes.

'Mr Tyler,' said the king, coldly. 'I gather that you are

demanding that I repeal the Poll Tax.'

'Erm…' said Tyler, looking a bit embarrassed. 'Actually, Your Majesty, we've changed our minds and chosen new demands via the new notes-on-trees democratic process. Our final demands are on this note.'

The king took the note from Tyler. It read:

1. Raise the horse speed limit to twelve miles an hour
2. Make St George's Day a Bank Holiday – I am ENGLISH and PROUD
3. Let's break a world record for the biggest note on a tree
4. Jeremy Clarkson for Prime Minister
5. Flemish imigrents need to respect OUR rules and OUR culture I am not a Rasist for saying so
6. I preferred the way notes on trees used to look BRING BACK THE OLD NOTES ON TREES

The king read Tyler's demands carefully, and nodded. Then, he did an incredibly brave thing. He spurred his horse forward and rode right into the peasants' camp, where he hammered a note of his own onto the tallest tree. It read:

'If a hundred thousand peasants join this note and return to their homes, I will concede to all their demands.'

A mighty cheer went up from the crowd and the men of Essex and Kent signed the note and began to pack up their things and disperse. It was harvest time and there was plenty to do at home, after all, especially with the world record attempt on the biggest tree note ever to look forward to. King Richard himself returned to the Tower, where, amid much feasting and joy, he began writing a new note.

'I bet I can hunt down and hang the hundred thousand idiots who believed me,' it began.

DICK WHITTINGTON AND HIS CAT

ONE SUNNY DAY IN THE YEAR 1370, A POOR BOY FROM Gloucester by the name of Dick Whittington crept out of his house at the crack of dawn to run away to London. He had heard that the streets there were paved with gold and he was determined to have some for himself. As he started walking, with the wind ruffling his mop of golden hair, Dick had little idea that he would one day become the greatest and most famous Lord Mayor that the city of London would ever know.

It was many days and many adventures before Dick reached the city. He was overcome by the sights and the smells of the place, but he was single-minded and he immediately set about looking for gold on the floor. At first, he found none, so he kept on looking and, by lunchtime, he found himself in the Soho area, where a pretty girl asked him what he was up to. When Dick told her that he was looking for gold, she asked him if he should like to take a break and come and see her in her house with no clothes on. Dick eagerly accepted, and he was soon sat at a table in a basement drinking a glass of cool water and watching the girl gyrate in nothing but her pants.

'This is the life,' thought Dick, 'and tomorrow I shall find the gold that will make me rich.'

At that moment a burly man-at-arms wearing a black overcoat came over to Dick and handed him a bill for two hundred groats. Dick thought there must be some mistake, for all he had consumed was a glass of water. The man-at-arms then took out a parchment and a quill pen and began to draw something on it.

'Whatever are you drawing?' said Dick.

'I'm drawing a picture of you with this naked girl,' said the man-at-arms. 'And unless you pay me, I'll send it to your parents. After I've finished beating the daylights out of you, that is.'

'Can I go out and find some gold quickly?' said Dick.

'No,' said the man-at-arms. 'You cannot. How would you

feel about dancing in your pants for some rich Saracens we've got coming along later?'

At this, Dick broke down and cried, and the naked girl took pity on him. She told him that her master was a rich merchant and that Dick could work in their kitchen until he had paid off the two hundred groats for his water. Sniffing and wiping his eyes, Dick agreed, and the next day he was taken to the house of a merchant named Mr Fitzwarren, who was a kindly man. Mr Fitzwarren put Dick to work in his kitchen, where he would learn to prepare rich merchant's dishes like braised rack of swan and hand-cut turnip chips.

Dick was safe and sound in the kitchen but his sleeping quarters were a problem: they were infested with mice, who would run over him and chew at his golden hair in the night. He resolved to buy a cat just as soon as he had paid for the glass of water, and that is what he did. He called her Fluffy and she did an excellent job of keeping mice out of Dick's room. One day, Mr Fitzwarren announced that he was sending a ship to faraway lands to trade, and asked his household if they wanted to send anything on his ship.

'I have nothing but my cat, sir,' said Dick. 'I will send Fluffy on board the ship – that should get me some money.'

'You mercenary little bastard,' Mr Fitzwarren frowned.

'Well… that's how I got where I am today, I suppose. You can put Fluffy on the ship.'

So Fluffy was stuffed into a small crate and sent away on Mr Fitzwarren's ship, and Dick went back to being chewed by mice in the night. He put up with this for weeks and then months until one day he decided to leave. He was fed up with London, where there was no gold on the streets after all. He packed up his possessions in a blue carrier bag and got on the number 43 horse and cart that went up Holloway Road. But just then a very strange thing happened. Dick heard the Bow Bells ringing, and it seemed to him that they were saying, 'Turn again, Whittington, thrice Mayor of London.'

Dick jumped off the cart and started running back. He leapt over tramps and dodged dog mess all the way back to Mr Fitzwarren's house, where he burst in, quite out of breath.

'Sir! Sir! Did the ship return, having sold Fluffy to a Far Eastern prince whose palace was overrun with mice and who paid an absolute fortune for it?' Dick panted.

'My word,' said the merchant. 'No wonder they call you Dick. The ship *has* returned, however. It appears that the captain swapped your cat for a ridiculous two-wheeled contraption called a bicycle that one of the natives invented. He kept getting knocked off it so he wanted rid of it.'

Mr Fitzwarren wheeled something out of his storeroom. It had two wheels, was made mostly of metal tubes and it had two pedals on it.

'What the hell am I supposed to do with that?' cried Dick. 'That won't keep mice out of my hair. I want my cat back! I'm going to the RSPCA at once to tell them everything!'

He took the odd-looking contraption, hopped onto it and wobbled off down the street, with everyone laughing at him. In that moment, Dick resolved to ride the bicycle right into the Thames and end it all. He pedalled faster and faster, clattering through the streets at a breakneck pace, wobbling dangerously with his golden hair flying about his head.

A mile down the road, he came to a square where the citizens of London were gathering to elect a new Lord Mayor, and they were arguing loudly because no one knew who the best man for the job would be. Then, Dick clattered into the square on his contraption and knocked over a stall of turnips and everyone turned to look.

'Let's elect him as Lord Mayor of London,' cried a costermonger.

'But he's just a buffoon with no experience of running a city such as this,' said a butcher.

'I don't care,' said the costermonger. 'Look at him wobbling around town on his contraption with his big mop of golden hair – it'll be brilliant!'

'Yeah… it would be pretty amusing,' said the butcher. 'Go on then – let's elect him.'

So, in this way, Dick did indeed become Lord Mayor, and he turned out to be such a good and popular Lord Mayor that the citizens elected him twice again, making him thrice Mayor of London and a very happy man indeed.

HENRY THE EIGHTH: LOVER, STONER, ENTREPRENEUR

N O ENGLISH KING CUTS A MORE FAMOUS AND FLAMBOYANT figure than Henry VIII. This multi-talented monarch excelled at almost everything he turned his hand to: warfare, statesmanship, music, sports, beheading people and getting married.

Henry was born into the high life and he lived it to the full. He spent great sums of money on archery, jousting, balls, hunting and fighting the French – but most of all, Henry loved to smoke the strong cannabis that the explorer Magellan had just brought back to Europe from a place called the Spice Islands somewhere in the eastern seas. Henry stashed his weed in the vast codpiece of his suit of armour to avoid it being

confiscated by his ministers, who disapproved of the effect
that it had on him. When under the influence, Henry got very
little done apart from giggling, eating and writing songs like
his classic composition *Greenleaves*, which still survives in an
altered form today.

> *Alas, my love, my eyes are red,*
> *That bong of skunk has done for me.*
> *Now I must stagger off to bed,*
> *Or I will vomit ferociously.*
> *Life is naught but bitches and money (repeat)*

Henry's habit began to create problems for the country. The
king was expected to produce an heir as quickly as possible
to continue his family line – but his permanently stoned and
befuddled state of mind meant that he was often incapable of
leaving the Tower of London unless it was to go to the twenty-
four-hour snack market next door. Worse still, it meant that
when he did venture out for the evening, he would find himself
attracted to the most unsuitable women. To the horror of his
ministers, Henry ended up getting married six times.

Henry's first wife was Katherine of Argos, the daughter of
a rich merchant who pioneered the selling of goods through

illuminated parchment catalogues. They met when Henry went down to her father's flagship store to find a lute 'with wicked bass tones' and it was love at first sight. The pair married in 1509 and lived happily until it was noticed that they had not produced an heir. An urgent investigation revealed that Katherine was allowing Henry to doze off on the sofa every night without fulfilling his matrimonial duties.

Against Henry's wishes, Katherine was quickly heaved aside for a new love interest: the enchanting Anne the Slag. The daughter of an ambitious country family, she was educated, refined and eager to produce an heir. Although Henry pointed out that Anne's nickname didn't really fill him with trust, his ministers arranged the marriage anyway. It lasted a year. Tragically for her, Anne was caught making advances to an undercover reporter disguised as the Sultan of Turkey.

After that experience, Henry decided that he needed a good, old-fashioned wife who would be loyal and could keep him in check. He soon met his match in Catherine the Strict, the strait-laced daughter of a country vicar. However, things soon began to go wrong. Catherine fell out with Henry after confronting him for coming home the worse for drink several nights running. In a fit of pique, Henry complained that this was worse than living with his mother. He spent the next month sleeping on the sofa at Cardinal Wolsey's house and swiftly obtained the first ever 'quickie' divorce.

It was while drowning his sorrows after this failed relationship that Henry met Anne of Summers in a Soho tavern and found himself drawn to this self-made and confident woman. The pair quickly set up a sensual love nest in an annexe of the Tower of London, with black velvet curtains and suggestive paintings on the walls. It seemed like bliss.

Then, one day, Henry returned from a smoking session with Thomas More to find Anne throwing a raucous, female-only party. As Henry stood in the doorway, aghast, Anne picked up a parsnip and began making lewd gestures with it before she realized from the shocked faces of her guests that the king had arrived home and was standing behind her.

From here things swiftly deteriorated for Henry. Katherine of Argos and Catherine the Strict had to be beheaded by on-stage security after fighting with each other and blaspheming at a royal tournament, and the constant strain of divorce settlements and custody battles began to take their toll on the king's mind. In 1547, Henry had to be coaxed down from the spire of Westminster Abbey, which he'd scaled wearing a Spiderman costume to demand better weekend access to the young Prince Edward.

By now, the once-dashing king had become grotesquely fat and spotty from a diet of fizzy drinks and swan-flavoured meat snacks. Nonetheless, he found himself the centre of attention when a Russian minstrel named Svetlana of Moscow came to town. She was all the rage amongst the people of London for her raunchy ballad 'I Want To Touch Your Codpiece', which had stormed the popular minstrel's charts and remained at number one for eight weeks. On her arrival in town she made a beeline for the vulnerable king. Henry was again smitten, and he went as far as to have several ministers beheaded for suggesting that the relationship wouldn't last. Nonetheless, Henry soon found himself unable to meet the demands of the voluptuous minstrel and, pretty soon, she left him.

After five divorces, the royal finances were in a state of absolute disarray. Henry needed cash and he needed it quickly. He went to his stash box for some weed to smoke while he pondered the situation but found it empty. This was a terrible annoyance for Henry. Buying the stuff in those days involved finding a merchant and then negotiating over the cost at length, for there were no fixed measures and no fixed prices. Suddenly, Henry had an ingenious idea.

The next day, he ordered every weed merchant in the kingdom beheaded and their heads placed on Tower Bridge.

Next, he called his ministers to his chambers and informed them that, from now on, he was in business as England's sole weed dealer. Inaccurate weights and measures like the 'handful' and the 'baggie' were to be done away with and replaced by a measure named after the king himself: the eighth.

Henry proved to be a shrewd businessman. He fixed the price of an eighth at three pence, except for first-time buyers, to whom he gave a discount in the hope of getting them hooked. He also banned the importation of the bookmaker William Caxton's new printed books to preserve the royal monopoly on rolling parchment, in which he did a roaring secondary trade. All of the weed smokers in London were soon flocking to the back door of the Tower and, within a year, Henry's finances were in rude health.

With this done, it only remained for Henry to find himself a sixth wife. As it happened, love awaited him around the corner in his favourite East London tavern, which had just had a change of management. Peggy of Windsor was a sprightly landlady with a heart of gold and a habit of giving Henry flagons of ale on the house. After a whirlwind courtship, during which Henry was nearly tempted away from Peggy by Pat of Walford, the pair settled down to a happy marriage and produced the son that Henry longed for.

Sadly the marriage was cut short when Henry wandered into the path of a speeding horse and cart on his way back from the twenty-four-hour market after an all-day smoking session – but his life's work was carried on by his son, who went on to deal weed in even greater quantities than his father and who eventually became King Edward the Quarter.

ELIZABETH I: THE VIRGIN QUEEN

QUEEN ELIZABETH WAS A WISE AND GRACIOUS QUEEN and her subjects knew her as Good Queen Bess. She loved to dress up in fine gowns and to knight adventurers on the decks of their ships – but she was harbouring a dark secret. Queen Elizabeth, ruler of the waves, was a virgin.

Of course, everyone called her the Virgin Queen but no one believed that it was true. These were the days before television, after all, when there was little else to do in the evenings. Her mother, Anne the Slag, Henry's second wife, had been at it from her teens – but poor Elizabeth had had little luck with men. The problem was that her dad was Henry VIII, who had threatened every one of Elizabeth's boyfriends with beheading if they so much as thought about getting to first base with his daughter; who personally waited on the doorstep of the Tower of London every night to vet his daughter's dates, picking his teeth with an axe as he did so. Even after Henry was long dead, the men of England were too frightened of him to ask his daughter out.

To make matters worse, Elizabeth had a rival – the hated Mary, Queen of Scots. As well as wanting the crown of England for herself, Mary wanted something else: Robert Dudley, Earl of Leicester and the object of Queen Elizabeth's affection. Dudley was an influential statesman, a great wit and, most importantly, was considered the fittest gentleman in Elizabeth's court. Elizabeth knew that he was the man to break her duck. Mary, meanwhile, knew that the queen wanted Dudley but was prepared to go all out to snag him for herself.

Shortly after Elizabeth was crowned, she hit upon the bright idea of inviting Dudley over to watch a couple of plays round at her palace. She spent the whole afternoon setting the mood with candles and nibbles and a minstrel singing relaxing songs. When Dudley arrived, she answered the door with her ruff suggestively undone and the pair sat down on her sofa to watch a racy thriller performed by an intimate cast of twelve actors. By the end of the third act, Elizabeth had manoeuvred herself up next to Dudley and as the play came to an end, she made her move and pretended to yawn, stretching her arms upright and placing one around Dudley's shoulder. At that moment there came a frantic knocking on the door.

It was Mary, Queen of Scots, who informed Elizabeth that a rebellion by the Northern Earls had just taken place. Elizabeth flew from her seat and summoned her ministers to form a council of war. When they arrived, however, they told her that there was no such rebellion. Elizabeth realized she had been tricked. When the panic subsided, she looked for Mary, but the Queen of Scots had made herself scarce – and Dudley had nodded off on the sofa. Although disheartened, Elizabeth was made of sterner stuff than to give up on Dudley and so the next day, she announced that she would throw a ball in his honour the following evening.

She dressed up for the occasion in a revealing outfit that left little to the imagination and Dudley did a double-take when he turned up and saw her. After a few lively numbers, Elizabeth commanded her orchestra to play 'Everything I Do' by the New World minstrel Bryane Adams, and she approached Dudley for a slow dance. They shuffled around slowly to the music, gazing into each other's eyes, and Dudley was about to ask Elizabeth whether she would like to go for a stroll outside when Mary tapped her on the shoulder, looking out of breath.

Mary informed Elizabeth that a religious crisis had developed and was threatening to engulf the realm. Elizabeth quickly stopped the music and began forming the Anglican church at once. Then, out of the corner of her eye, she saw that Mary was flirting with Dudley and giggling loudly and she was sure that she heard the word 'virgin'. Mary had tricked her again. In a rage, Elizabeth stormed out of the hall, leaving Dudley chatting to her bitter rival.

The next day, Elizabeth took to desperate measures, pulling out her make-up box and making herself up as suggestively as possible with an inch of corrosive white lead foundation and false eyelashes. When her minister Lord Cecil tactfully suggested that 'Your Majestie hath a bodie off Bayewatch yet a face off Crymewatche', she had him stretched on the rack for his insolence and piled the foundation on even thicker.

That evening, Elizabeth left nothing to chance and downed two bottles of wine before sending a perfume-drenched messenger over to Dudley's asking what he was up to. Her intentions were obvious and Dudley turned up quickly, clutching some flowers from a late-night market stall. Elizabeth steeled her nerve and prepared to lunge at Dudley to seal the deal once and for all, but, as she did so, there came a knock on the door. Yet again it was Mary, Queen of Scots, who told Elizabeth that a great Armada was on its way from Spain that would scatter the English in its wake. This time, however, Elizabeth was having none of it. She called for her guards and had Mary dragged away to be tried for treason and executed.

'That was an over-reaction,' moaned Dudley, walking out.

'I have the body of a weak and feeble woman,' cried Elizabeth, 'and it's totally hot for you! Take me, Sir Robert!'

Dudley stopped and turned on his heel at once. Elizabeth gazed into his eyes and she saw that he felt the same way. Dudley bounded forwards, swept Elizabeth up in his arms and kissed her tenderly across every inch of her face – and dropped down dead.

'Bloody lead-based make-up,' sighed Elizabeth. 'Oh well… the Virgin Queen it is.'

Sir Francis Drake and the Armada Language School

FRANCIS DRAKE WAS *THE* MAN OF HIS DAY. BY THE 1580s, the fearless adventurer and seadog had plundered Spain's harbours and colonies around the world, seized ships full of South American gold and silver, circumnavigated the globe, claimed California for England and been knighted by Queen Elizabeth on board his ship the *Golden Hind*. Every man wanted to be in his crew and many ladies would giggle coyly at him. But one day in 1588, everything changed.

After a busy few months of raising hell on the high seas, Drake docked his ship at Chatham and his crew went their separate ways to spend their plunder on a summer of beer and women. Drake himself headed for Plymouth, where he planned to spend an afternoon with an infamous woman of ill-repute known only as the Plymouth Ho, who had a reputation as a girl who would do just about anything for a gentleman who took her ten-pin bowling at the local Bowl-Me-Ova lanes. Drake galloped his horse down to Plymouth, gave himself a quick squirt of a fine cologne that he'd plundered from a Spanish galleon, picked up the Plymouth Ho and trotted straight to Bowl-Me-Ova.

However, something was clearly amiss. Although Drake paid admission for them both, held doors open for her, bought her drinks and sweets and impressed her by scoring several strikes, he sensed that the Plymouth Ho wasn't that interested. Undeterred, he paid for another game, after which he bought lunch, sat next to her, stretched and put his arm around her – only to have her slap his hand away. At last, Drake could take no more and confronted her.

'I am the greatest maritime adventurer in the world,' Drake cried, 'and yet you are not attracted to me? Is it the cologne? I *knew* it was a bit poncey but that Spanish bastard assured me that…'

'No, sir,' interjected the Plymouth Ho. 'You are most charming and kind and you smell very nice, but it is almost August and the Spanish are coming.'

'They are coming with an army to invade?' asked Drake. 'Why do I not know this?'

'Not an invasion, silly – the Armada Language School!' said the Plymouth Ho. 'Hundreds of thousands of Spanish students are coming to England for the summer to learn English and loads of them are staying in Plymouth. My word, but they are sexy and romantic – they are so dark and handsome. I can't wait to do it with one of them under the pier. They won't even have to take me bowling!'

Drake's hand shot to the hilt of his rapier.

'I should cut you down for your insolence,' he growled. 'I, Sir Francis Drake, am several quid out of pocket and have spent the whole afternoon in a bloody bowling alley and you have not given me as much as a kiss with tongues. I shall finish this game and then I shall thrash the Armada Language School and then – THEN – you will put out.'

But even as he spoke, the Plymouth Ho let out a great squeal for there, on the horizon, were the ships of the Armada Language School – hundreds of them. They gave off an eerie yellow glow from the thousands of neon-rucksack-wearing language students that swarmed their decks in packs of thirty or more. Below him, Drake could see all the girls of Plymouth making their way to the seafront to welcome the invaders. He leapt on his horse and spurred it all the way back to London, where he rounded up his crew.

'Gentlemen,' cried Drake, 'we must defeat the Spaniards, 'ere they shag all the women – including Good Queen Bess.'

To a roar of approval, the *Golden Hind* put out to sea to meet the enemy head-on for a sea battle. To their horror, however, they reached Plymouth to find that the Armada Language School had already landed. They were too late and would now face a terrible land battle against a numerically superior foe. Drawing their swords, the Englishmen rushed off the *Hind* and onto the beach but found that they could barely move for the numbers of language students.

They were everywhere, milling around in large huddles, shouting, screaming and playing Frisbee without regard for any of the poor locals who could do little but tut disapprovingly under the onslaught. Wherever the English turned they found more of their foe, many playing rock chords on battered guitars with their friends cheering them on. On the seafront, the Spaniards besieged shops attempting to buy booze underage and laughed at the shopkeepers who refused them. Worse, the girls of Plymouth were absolutely lapping it up.

Drake held his rapier aloft and led a valiant charge. He only managed to get a few yards before he tripped over the size fifteen shoes of one seven-foot-tall student who sniggered cruelly at the English hero as he lay in the sand. The day seemed lost. If the students could be split into smaller groups they could be dealt with but their number was too great.

Already, several local girls had been chatted up by the invaders and one was already heavy petting with a young man in a bandanna underneath the pier. Drake's group battled their way to the shops on the seafront to regroup, where they hunkered down outside a store that sold penknives and drugs paraphernalia to make their next move. Just then, Drake spotted an ice-cream cart and had a flash of inspiration.

As fast as they could, Drake and his men loaded the ice-cream cart with as many bongs, pipes, outsized cigarette papers and comedy lighters as they could, throwing in a few T-shirts with marijuana leaf designs and several lit firecrackers for good measure. Then they rolled the cart straight into the mass of language students. As the students heard the firecrackers going off and spotted the super-cool contents of the cart, pandemonium broke out. Every one of them wanted the contents of the cart and set about trying to grab it. By now, the cart was travelling too fast for any of them to halt it; although several threw themselves under the wheels, the cart rolled straight over them and onto the pier.

The language students followed the cart in a great mass, whooping and yelling and waving their guitars over their heads. Suddenly, there was a great creaking and groaning from the pier. Overloaded with language students, it swayed left and then right before giving way completely, coming down with a crash into the sea. Not a single language student was left on the beach.

'You wankers,' screamed the girls, who ran down to the sea only to find that the students of the Armada Language School had perished to a man. Drake and the men of England were triumphant.

'Now to find that Plymouth Ho,' said Drake with a hearty

chuckle. Smug with victory, he made his way to the bowling alley, treated the Plymouth Ho to a huge bucket of ice cream and promenaded her back to his lodgings as the townspeople cheered and applauded.

'Strike!' smiled Francis Drake.

WALTER RALEIGH: SOCIAL CLIMBER

WALTER RALEIGH WAS A HANDSOME YOUNG SAILOR from Devon with big ambitions. He lived during an age when England had no king, just a Virgin Queen, Elizabeth, and he dreamed of one day marrying the queen and the two of them making several little Raleigh princes and princesses.

Everyone derided him for his dream, for he was a commoner and the queen only hung out with knights of the realm or higher, but he clung on to the fantasy. One day, he made up his mind to go to London and do something so gallant that Queen Elizabeth would knight him there and then and he could ask her out on a date.

He wasn't sure what sort of gallant thing to do, so he followed Queen Elizabeth around London wherever she went, waiting for a mugger to try to steal her jewels or for a runaway cart to roll towards her or for any other situation where he could display his gallantry. Then one day, it happened. It was January, the sales were on and Queen Elizabeth was doing a spot of bargain-hunting on Oxford Street. Suddenly, she found a great puddle in her path – a really filthy one full of spit and dead pigeons. Quick as a flash, Raleigh sprinted forwards, whipped off his cloak and threw it onto the puddle for her to walk upon. When she was across, she looked at Raleigh, clearly impressed.

'Such behaviour is worthy of… a knight,' said Queen Elizabeth. 'What is your name, handsome stranger?'

'My name is Walter…' began Raleigh in the poshest accent he could put on, but then there was a huge commotion from down the road and the sound of galloping hooves approached. It was the great hero and knight of the realm Sir Francis Drake.

'Majesty,' said Drake. 'Allow me to present you with this bag of gold that I just plundered from a Spanish galleon. Please take it as a humble token of my esteem.'

'Good sir,' said Raleigh as politely as he could. 'I was talking to Her Majesty before you were.'

'Piss off, chav,' growled Drake. 'I see what you're up to. However, the only gallantry that Her Maj is interested in is plundering Spanish galleons for gold. If you can't give Her Majesty a handful of booty, you can forget about a knighthood and you can forget about *her* majestic booty. Get it?'

'It's true,' sighed Queen Elizabeth. 'There's something just so gallant about plundering a galleon with extreme violence and giving me a load of gold. Anyway – see you later. I'm off for a pizza with Sir Francis.'

And with that, they were off. Raleigh retrieved his cloak from the puddle. It was covered in big, gloopy clots of pigeon feather and phlegm.

'I *will* become Sir Walter Raleigh,' Raleigh muttered under his breath. 'I *will*.'

Raleigh went home, scraped together all the money he could, took out several high-interest loans and sold his horse in order to buy a small, secondhand ship out of the back of the *Plymouth Mercury*. He formed a crew and announced that he was off to the New World to plunder the Spanish treasure fleet.

After several months at sea, however, there was no sign of a Spanish treasure fleet. All that Raleigh could find along the coast of the New World were lots of villages full of natives who rolled up bundles of leaves and smoked them. Raleigh searched and searched for Spanish ships but he found none. He was at his wits' end and getting grumpier and grumpier. One day, he became so annoyed and fed up that he went ashore and smoked leaves with the natives, which gave him an idea.

Six months later, Walter Raleigh knocked on the door of the queen's palace dressed in the finest silks and carrying a heavy pouch that jingled when he walked. The news was reported to Elizabeth, who requested that she see him at once.

'Your Majesty,' cried Raleigh, bowing low. 'Allow me to present you with this bag of gold that I plundered – personally – from a Spanish galleon.'

'Tell me more!' said Elizabeth, a faint blush appearing on her cheeks. 'Can you smell smoke, by the way?'

'No, I can't,' said Raleigh with a cough. 'Anyway, so I was sailing along and there were these three Spanish ships to my one ship, and they got lippy, all like, "What are you looking at, *sir*?" and I was like, "Come on, then," and it kicked off. I sank one of the ships with my sword, and then I decked some conquistadors, and one captain was all: "Please, no… *sir*…" but I decked him anyway, and the others all ran off, and then I…'

'Enough,' said Elizabeth, a great grin on her face. 'You will be made a knight at once, Mr Raleigh, and propelled to the very top of Elizabethan society. And then we shall go on a date.'

'Sweet!' Raleigh cried. 'Shall we do the knighting here, or...'

'Not so hasty, sir,' said Elizabeth. 'Come back next week with lots more gold from your plunders and we'll do it then.'

Raleigh left the palace with a whoop of joy and galloped back to Plymouth. Elizabeth watched him go and then realized that she'd forgotten to ask him his sword size for the knighting. With time on her hands, she decided to ride down to Plymouth to ask Raleigh in person – and maybe catch a glimpse of his treasure ship. She disguised herself with a hood, hopped on a horse and trotted down to the West Country incognito to find Raleigh, which she found all rather romantic.

Plymouth was all of a bustle when the queen arrived and there was a great crowd of people down by the docks. Elizabeth decided to stop off there and get a couple of tins of cider for her and Raleigh to drink. It was true that he wasn't a knight yet but he did seem very noble. As she made her way through the busy streets, she saw a figure standing on top of an overloaded white wagon waving a bag of something that looked like leaves, and decided to take a closer look. It appeared to be Raleigh. Surely he was recounting his daring raid on the Spanish galleon, Elizabeth thought, and she pushed closer to hear.

'Two ounces – just two ounces for a gold paaahnd,' Raleigh was yelling through a smouldering bundle of leaves that he had in his mouth. Elizabeth was puzzled. The cart was surrounded by rough-looking men holding gold coins – coins similar to those that Raleigh had presented to her.

'Duty-free fags,' Raleigh shouted, his face red with yelling. 'Virginia tobacco, duty free! Fresh off the boat and SCREW the taxman. Come on, people. I need gold pieces quickly so I'm positively giving this stuff away. Cuttin' me own throat.

Come on. This stuff's fackin' brilliant. Roll up, roll up and gimme your gold: I've got a crack at getting in the royal pants but first I've gotta straighten some fackin' lie about a treasure ship I didn't plunder. Roll up!'

'Mr Raleigh!' shrieked Queen Elizabeth, and the marketplace went very quiet indeed.

Walter Raleigh was beheaded in 1618 after a lengthy, non-smoking imprisonment.

THE GENIUS OF WILLIAM SHAKESPEARE

I N 1592, WILLIAM SHAKESPEARE WAS A STRUGGLING YOUNG playwright with a problem. His latest play had closed after just one week due to poor attendance figures. Audiences hated *Hamlet* and Shakespeare was fuming – not to mention broke. He could barely afford to keep himself in quill pens, and final demands for bills were piling up fast on his doormat.

'It's too intellectual,' said his agent, a short man with a toupee. 'I keep telling you – people want to see drama that reflects real, gritty life. The theatre-going public don't want to hear a pampered prince moaning about his mum.'

'Fine,' said Shakespeare. 'I've got a new idea anyway: two young lovers born into feuding noble families, who…'

'There you go again,' said his agent. 'Rich kids complaining about their lives. What's next – a duke with glandular fever? Look, Bill, we need to write something real, down-to-earth. Believable – you know? Listen up – I want you to write something set in a gritty East London slum and make it as grim as possible, otherwise you're going to end up shovelling horse manure for a living.'

With that, the agent walked out, leaving Shakespeare sitting at his shabby desk, quietly seething.

'Bloody philistine,' he muttered. 'I'll show him. I'll write something so tediously grim it's unreal. *Then* let him tell me it's what audiences want to watch while they're having their tea.'

He dipped his pen in the inkpot and he began to write.

Who shot Phil: that is the question:
Whether 'tis nobler in the mind to suspect Mark Fowler,
Who resented him for his slings and arrows against Lisa,
Or to take arms against Ian Beale,
Who was after all in the bushes when Phil was popped;
And, by opposing, ended Phil's relationship with Kathy, Ian's
    mum.
Although Phil did contribute a bit by shagging Sharon.
Also Kathy got off with Grant, I think,

Before he went to the New World. Slag. To die, to sleep.
To sleep; and then to make a brief comeback last year.
For in that sleep of death what dreams may come
Including the possibility that it was him out of Spandau Ballet
Whose realization that Phil had slept with Mel
Must give us pause. Didn't she sleep with Ian as well?
And help out in the chip shop? Ay, there's the pub,
Which Dan Sullivan and Phil did battle over.
And Dan would not bear the whips and scorns of Peggy,
And was, after all, seen in the phone box just beforehand.
But what of the Slater sisters? And Nick Cotton?
The plot has turned awry and lost all semblance of sense and;
I much preferred the era of Dirty Den, Sharon's dad
Who I believe is doing panto in Eastbourne.

He folded the page up, put it in an envelope, posted it to his agent and sloped off to the pub to spend his last few coins on beer. The next day, he was woken by a frantic hammering on the door. His agent was standing outside, waving the script.

'I love it,' the little man cried. 'When can you write the rest of it?'

'You can't love it,' Shakespeare scowled. 'It's bloody ridiculous.'

'The Globe want it,' said the agent, jumping up and down. 'The biggest theatre in all London want it and they'll pay you a hundred quid up front.'

'A hundred quid?' said Shakespeare. 'When do you need it by?'

Something is Rotten in the State of Wall-forde was a wildfire hit. Night after night, the Globe Theatre was packed to the rafters as the people of London flocked to see Shakespeare's gritty play. It ran for six whole months and sold out almost every day, and Shakespeare paid off his outstanding bills and even bought himself a new desk.

'I've got a new idea,' he said to his agent one day. 'It's about Antony and Cleopatra and it explores themes of…'

'Are you mad?' said the agent. 'The public want more East End grittiness. Get to work on the next instalment – this is going to run and run.'

Shakespeare sighed, sat down and started writing more.

His agent was right – *Wall-forde* ran and ran and spawned a new interest in the theatre: the Golden Age of Gritty Elizabethan Drama. Its actors became stars and were rarely off the front pages of the news pamphlets. The public went into a frenzy when bad-boy actor Grunt Michel defected to the rival Bearpit Theatre to play the lead role in *Ultimate Men-at-Arms*,

an even grittier piece of work about elite soldiers in the Low
Countries.

The popular teenage publications of the day competed for
the right to publish pictures of Shakespeare's female characters
in their underwear and the news pamphlets competed hard to
find strumpets and wenches who had enjoyed relations with
the actors before they became famous.

Many great actors of the day started their careers in *Wall-
forde*. Several left to 'break the New World', often with little
success. In most cases, they were reduced to playing in smaller,

so-called 'satellite theatres' where they were forced to eat insects and animal waste until they could take no more and begged for their old employers to 'get me out of here'. Viewed as hilarious at the time, the practice was eventually outlawed in 1602 when the actor Robert Deangaffnye choked to death on an elephant's testicle in front of a baying mob in Southwark.

The 1605 Christmas special of *Wall-forde* attracted the highest viewing figures of any play on record, due to a sensational plotline in which a servant wench murdered her employer with a mop handle. Shakespeare's fame was secured. His series had run for thirteen years and he decided that enough was enough. He devised a spectacular finale in which the Queen Maud burned down during an argumentative late-night lock-in with the entire cast inside – and then he left London quietly, lugging a trunk full of gold, to work on something a bit more intellectual.

Guy Fawkes and the Gunpowder Plot

Remember, remember, the fifth of November
Gunpowder, bangers and kitty
What sort of vile berk would place a lit firework
Into a cat? That's just gritty.

(ANON)

GUY FAWKES WAS A VERY MISCHIEVOUS YOUNG MAN AND a very good example of what happens when boys give in to peer pressure.

Fawkes was born into the Catholic gentry at a time when England, under King James VI, was Protestant. Not that this mattered to the young Fawkes a jot – he just wanted to be a part of Robert Catesby's gang. Catesby was the leader of a group of local boys in Fawkes's village who hung around after school getting up to mischief. Everyone looked up to Robert Catesby. He was the oldest of the gang and was tall enough to purchase cider in the local shop.

One day, Catesby returned from a family holiday to France

and the gang were sitting in their local park smoking cigarettes. Suddenly, a huge bang went off behind them and they found themselves covered in vile-smelling sludge. Catesby had inserted a French banger into a cowpat. The boys wailed and cursed for some time until Catesby opened his jacket to reveal a vast cache of illegal fireworks that he had smuggled through customs.

That evening, the gang went on a firework rampage. Francis Tresham placed a banger in an empty bottle and detonated it outside the local pub, while Thomas Bates put one in the coin slot of the telephone box. Soon, everybody had blown something up – everyone except Guido Fawkes. Fawkes was worried that his dad would come outside and ground him, so he hung around at the back of the group egging everyone else on, rather than blowing anything up himself. This did not go unnoticed.

'Willst thou blow something up, Guido,' smirked Robert Catesby. 'Or should I say... Gay-do?'

Guido Fawkes felt his blood boil. He hated his parents for naming him that anyway, which was why he called himself Guy instead, and to have his hero mock him in such a manner made him even more resentful.

'I am not afraid to blow something up, sir,' said Guido.

'Do a cat, then,' said Catesby. 'I bet thou wouldst not.'

'A cat?' said Guido. 'That's sick.'

'Gay-do, Gay-do,' chanted Catesby, and soon the rest of the gang joined in.

'Fine,' said Fawkes. 'Give me a banger and I shall do it.'

The gang spent the rest of the evening roaming the village looking for a cat, but they could not find one, and this secretly made Guy Fawkes very relieved. He shrugged his shoulders and said that he would certainly have done the deed if they had found a cat, and, with that, he started walking home, for it was past his curfew.

'Fear not, Guido,' said Catesby. 'We shall find one on our school trip to the Houses of Parliament tomorrow.'

Fawkes's blood ran cold. He had forgotten about the annual school trip to London. The place would surely be teeming with cats. He barely slept that night, and when dawn came, he placed his face on the radiator to fake a temperature and told his mother that he had a terrible stomach ache. His mother, however, was having none of it, and she packed Guy off on the horse and cart to London, where his gang of friends were waiting for him with the rest of the bangers and some matches.

Fawkes spent a miserable morning on the way to London, knowing what his friends would make him do when they got there. He didn't even join in when they hung lewd woodcuts off the back of the cart so that horsemen would swerve in the road when they saw them, nor did he share their excitement when they wondered if the gift shop would have penknives. All he could do was hope that they wouldn't run into any cats for the whole day.

Luck was not on Guy Fawkes's side. The school had timed its visit to coincide with a state visit by King James himself, and, as they crowded the public viewing gallery of the House of Commons, Guy's stomach churned. King James had brought with him a large, ginger cat to give the Parliament as a mascot. All of Guido's gang saw it too, and when the king had gone and the school party was given half an hour to visit the gift shop before reporting back to the horse and cart, they bundled Fawkes off to find the cat.

'It will be in the cellars catching rats,' whispered a pale boy called Ambrose Rokewood, who had already proved himself by poking a banger through the letterbox of an elderly spinster the night before. The gang sneaked past a security guard and crept down to the cellars where, sure enough, they saw the king's ginger cat.

'Well, Guido?' said Catesby.

'I think we should go to the gift shop,' said Guido. 'We'll all get busted down here and be in detention for weeks. What say I prove myself by buying a penknife instead?'

'Gay-do,' whispered Ambrose Rokewood, and the other boys began to whisper it too. Guido felt his face flush. 'Gay-do,' the boys whispered, and something in him snapped. He grabbed a banger in one hand, grabbed the cat in the other and attempted to insert the banger into the wretched animal's back passage, which caused the cat to scratch him very hard across the face, which in turn caused Guido to howl in pain and the other boys to laugh very hard indeed.

Suddenly, the cellar door swung open. There, looking distinctly unamused, was King James, who had come down to say goodbye to the cat – and behind him was an entire detachment of guards.

'Guido Fawkes was trying to place a banger in the royal cat's bottom,' Robert Catesby squealed in a very high and scared voice. Catesby's betrayal of Guy was no use: the whole gang was seized and bundled outside for a public hanging, drawing and quartering. Word quickly spread amongst the townspeople, who turned out in their hundreds to watch the show. The rest of Catesby's bangers were loaded on top of a hastily built bonfire, where they exploded as the townspeople looked on, gorging themselves on fast food from a local burger cart. As the miscreants wriggled and screamed on the execution scaffold, everyone agreed that they couldn't remember the last time they'd had so much fun.

'This could be a good tradition,' thought King James, and he declared that, forthwith, every fifth of November would be devoted to letting off fireworks, gorging on burgers and worrying animals with bangers.

ROUNDHEADS AND CHAVALIERS

In THE YEAR 1640, PARLIAMENT FACED A SERIOUS PROBLEM: what to do about the behaviour of the young king, Charles I. He had fallen in with a group of trouble-making ruffians known as the Chavaliers, who had made him their leader. Charles and his Chavaliers wore bright, flashy clothes, peaked caps and copious quantities of gold jewellery and they loved nothing more than to get drunk and make a nuisance of themselves, mocking anyone without a peaked cap and calling them a 'roundhead'.

While his father James had been a wise, scholarly king, his eldest son Charles was quite the opposite. He had never paid attention at school, preferring to play truant and smoke his

tobacco pipe behind the stables and had been marched home by the city guards several times for drunkenly flinging bottles at boats from London Bridge. Now, the troublesome youth had become king.

Charles's first act as king had been to summon Parliament and demand money for him and his Chavaliers to get drunk. Parliament had agreed to pay him a sum of beer money every week, thinking that this was the best way to keep Charles out of their hair. The strategy had worked for a while – but now, Charles wanted something else.

It was a misty morning in November and Parliament was going about its business when there was a loud knock on the door. An MP called Oliver Cromwell grumpily shuffled across the room and opened the door – but there was no one there. Then, he looked down. A brown paper bag was burning on the doorstep. Cromwell shrugged and stamped the flames out. A howl of laughter rose from beyond the door. The bag was full of dog mess. With a cry of anguish, Cromwell stumbled back into the room and attempted to pick his sole clean with a twig but at that moment, the doors flew open and King Charles rode in at the head of a gang of Chavaliers.

'What is the meaning of this?' Cromwell cried. 'You have beshitten my good boots, Your Majesty.'

'Good boots?' the king yelled. 'They do not have a single stripe, nor an air bubble. You dress like an arse. Hold your tongue before I have my Chavaliers fling your shitty boots onto the Parliament roof. Now look at this!'

He unfurled a magazine and waved it in front of Cromwell's face.

'Sexy Nellie and Molly invite you into their penthouse hovel?' said Cromwell. 'I do not understand.'

'No, dolt!' yelled Charles. 'This!' He pointed to an article entitled 'King Bling' which featured the newly crowned king of

France wearing a huge golden crown studded with rubies.

'I want one of these,' said the king, 'and I command you to raise the necessary funds. I can't have this mug showing me up. I want a crown that's even bigger and I want diamonds in it, innit. So get taxing the people.'

'We can't just tax the people,' said Cromwell. 'We'd have to have a debate and take a vote on it. These things take time.'

'I see,' sulked King Charles. 'Well, give me your dinner money then.'

'I haven't got any,' said Cromwell. 'I brought sandwiches.'

Charles snapped his fingers. Several burly Chavaliers surrounded Cromwell, drew their swords and commanded him to jump up and down. When a faint jingling was heard, the Chavaliers grabbed him by his feet, held him upside down and shook him until several coins fell from his pockets.

'Line up!' the king shouted. The MPs formed a line and every man was made to jump up and down. Anyone who jingled was turned upside down and their pockets emptied. After an hour, the king had collected several hundred pounds and rode away with his Chavaliers, leaving Parliament angry, red-faced and without any dinner money.

The next day, Parliament was going about its business again when there was another knock on the door. Cromwell went to answer it and again saw a flaming plastic bag. This time, however, he was ready. Earlier that day, he had filled a bucket with water and he bent down to pick the bag up rather than stamping on it. As he bent down, however, two pairs of hands appeared from outside, grabbed the waistband of his underpants and heaved it upwards. With a scream, Cromwell was hoisted, wriggling, off the ground and King Charles swaggered in wearing the largest gold crown that anyone had ever seen. The Chavaliers hauled Cromwell inside and held him struggling in the middle of the chamber.

'What do you want this time, Majesty?' he whispered through gritted teeth.

'There's something missing off this crown,' said the king. 'What do you think it is?'

'I don't know, sire,' Cromwell said, clutching his chafed buttocks.

'A PEAK!' screamed the king. 'Fuck's sake! How am I supposed to get the respect that is due if my crown doesn't have a diamond-encrusted peak for me to wear at a jaunty angle? I'll look like one of you bloody no-peak roundheads – so rustle me up some dollars… now!'

'I've told you,' said Cromwell. 'We can't tax the country whenever you want something. Due process must be observed.'

'I've a process that I'd like you to observe,' said the king. 'Gentlemen: behold the Atomic Wedgie.'

The Chavaliers holding Cromwell's pants bent down and then leapt upwards, stretching the waistband of his pants right up to his neck and then hooking it over his head. Cromwell wailed and dropped to the floor, his spine locked, powerless to do anything but bend back and forth at the waist in a vain attempt to free himself.

'The rest of you…' roared King Charles, 'JUMP!'

As one, the Members of Parliament leapt to their feet and began jumping for fear that they too would suffer the Atomic Wedgie. The chamber was filled with the sound of coins jingling and the Chavaliers went around and emptied each man's pockets until the king had enough for his diamond-encrusted peak. Eventually the king and his Chavaliers left, and Cromwell was freed from his torment, although his underpants were permanently ruined.

The next day, the knock on the door came again. This time, Cromwell didn't open it; rather, he bent down and carefully peered through the peephole, where he saw something gold moving very quickly. Suddenly, a fist with lots of gold rings on it crashed through the wood and into his teeth.

'Look at these,' said King Charles, bounding through the

door. His crown now had a diamond-encrusted peak three feet high but the king seemed more interested in the gold rings on his hand.

'I've invented these,' he barked. 'Big gold rings with my face on them. As I'm your royal sovereign, I've named them Sovereign Rings and I want you to get me lots of gold to make ten each for all of my mates. Actually – why don't you just start jumping? Come on – JUMP!'

The king began to jump up and down threateningly and, out of fear, several of the Members of Parliament started to do so as well. Suddenly, the peak of the king's crown came loose and fell off. Charles dived to catch it but he fumbled, and as the cap fell to earth its peak landed on his throat. The diamonds on the peak of the cap sliced straight through his neck and the king's head rolled across the floor of Parliament.

Everybody stood very quietly for some time. At last, the Speaker piped up.

'What the hell are we going to say happened in here?' he wailed. 'There's royal blood all over the carpet and the king's dead.'

'I have an idea,' said Oliver Cromwell. 'We'll say he started a long and bloody civil war and we executed him when we won it.'

'Hmmm…' said the Speaker. 'No one's going to buy it.'

'Sure they will,' said Cromwell, clapping an arm around the Speaker's shoulders. 'Now – let's get this crown melted down and purchase ourselves a great big slap-up lunch!'

And, at this, the Members of Parliament all cheered, and off they ran to the canteen with their stomachs rumbling and Cromwell in the lead.

Charles II: The Merry Monarch

A T NOON, HOME TO DINNER, WHERE *I* DID FIND MY CARRIAGE *crushed by a piano fallen from a great height. I had occasion to fly into a rage and strike all around with my cane, whereupon the nearest officer of the watch approached and removed a false beard, revealing himself to be none other than the King. After swearing several times, I admitted that I could not believe it. Hilarity ensued, and so to bed.*

SAMUEL PEPYS'S DIARY, JANUARY 1663

Of all the kings and queens of England, none was so merry as Charles II, the Merry Monarch. Charles found joy in everything – mostly in playing elaborate pranks on his subjects.

The son of Charles I, who was mysteriously executed for starting a civil war, Charles II was forced to spend his youth in exile, travelling from royal court to royal court in Europe – and it was here that he learned of the joy of pranks. One day, travelling from the Dutch court to the French court, the young Charles realized at customs that in his bag were several hardcore pornographic prints purchased at the Amsterdam coach station. Panicking as his party approached the checkpoint, Charles had a brainwave and slipped the prints into his manservant's luggage. The servant was seized roughly and taken to the town square to be flogged.

Overcome with guilt, Charles ran after the customs officers and told them that he had planted the prints on the servant as a prank. To his surprise, everybody started laughing and patting the young prince on the back for such a clever jape – and the customs officers even let Charles keep the prints, although his mother later made him throw them away. That day, Charles resolved that when he gained the throne that was rightfully his, he would organize many, many more such pranks.

When he was allowed to return to England and become king, Charles took to London life with gusto. Every night he would go out drinking and whoring and would round off the evening with a prank. One night, he replaced a poor baker's horse and cart with an identical one and arranged for a piano to be dropped on it out of a window. As the baker wept and howled at the loss of his livelihood, the king arrived on the scene dressed as a blind piano tuner. When the baker eventually stopped sobbing, he couldn't help but see the funny side.

Charles organized one particularly famous jape at the hanging, drawing and quartering of the traitor Thomas Harrison. As Harrison wriggled on the scaffold, Charles donned filthy rags and a large leather hood to disguise himself as the executioner. He strung Harrison up, cut him down while still alive, cut off his genitals, disembowelled him – and then removed his executioner's hood to reveal himself. Harrison was initially furious but could not help laughing. 'I doth not believe it,' were the traitor's final, gurgled words as he expired of blood loss and shock.

In 1665, Charles hit upon his greatest ruse yet. Hearing that the Dutch ambassador was arriving for a state visit to town, he summoned his guards, dressed them up as dock workers and high-tailed it down to the docks where the ambassador's carriage was being unloaded. Charles himself was dressed as a bearded harbourmaster and greeted the ambassador warmly to distract him while his men got into position.

At the king's signal, the guards gave the carriage a shove down the gangplank, and the Dutch ambassador watched in horror as the carriage careered off the edge and splashed into the filthy Thames. Charles could barely contain himself as the ambassador swore and raged. However, before he could reveal himself, the ambassador stamped onto his ship and sailed off.

The next thing Charles knew, a vengeful Dutch fleet had sailed up the Thames and were bombarding Chatham Dockyard. His prank had inadvertently sparked the second Anglo-Dutch war, and his ministers were furious. The Dutch ambassador eventually saw the funny side when Charles turned up at Chatham dressed as an ugly fishwife complete with outrageous fake warts. After uttering several swear words which had to be drowned out with a trumpet, the ambassador laughed and called the war off. Even so, Charles decided that it was time to lay off the pranks for a while.

However, the king's enthusiasm for pranks couldn't be tamed for long, and in 1666, he thought of an even greater wheeze. The plague was raging in London and he knew that the citizens needed cheering up, so, in the middle of the night, he dressed up as a baker's apprentice and crept down to Pudding Lane in the middle of the old city. There, he lit a candle and dropped it into a pile of straw before tiptoeing away – barely able to stifle his giggles – to get dressed up as a bearded Chief of the Fire Brigade. When he arrived back on the scene, however, he found that his prank had been more effective than he had bargained for. Charles had started the Great Fire of London – the city was now ablaze and screams rang out through the streets.

I rode down to the waterside and there saw a lamentable fire, wrote diarist Samuel Pepys. *Everybody was endeavouring to remove their goods; poor people staying in their houses as long as till the very fire touched them, and then running into boats. And to top it all, I saw the Chief of the Fire Brigade, a man with a particularly ridiculous beard, running AWAY from the fire towards the Royal Palace. What a fucking disgrace.*

The Merry Monarch had finally taken things too far – and he knew it. After creeping back into the palace, he summoned his closest ministers to his chambers and bade them be seated.

'Gentlemen,' said the king, pacing up and down the room. 'My practical jokes have finally become intolerable. Forthwith, I will hang up my prankster's boots and will derive my merriment only from wine, women and song.'

'This is truly a sad day, Your Majesty,' the chief minister said. 'Nonetheless, I feel that you have made the correct decision.'

'Thank you,' said Charles, solemnly. 'I have at last seen the error of my ways. Gentlemen, please go with my thanks.'

The ministers nodded and rose to leave, only to find themselves stuck to their chairs with fast-drying glue.

'Gotcha,' said the Merry Monarch.

DICK TURPIN: CHARITY MUGGER EXTRAORDINAIRE

IN THE 1730s, ONE NAME STRUCK TERROR INTO TRAVELLERS the length and breadth of the land: Dick Turpin, the notorious highwayman, brigand and collector for a variety of good causes. His notorious cry of 'Stand and deliver!' caused hundreds if not thousands of men to tremble – rooted to the spot – and caused hundreds of ladies' hearts to flutter.

Born plain Richard Turpin in Essex, Turpin didn't choose a life of accosting travellers for a living. As a young man, he dreamed of becoming an actor in one of London's famous theatres; however, despite years of auditions, he failed to get so much as a walk-on role as a pickpocket in the play *The Bow Street Runners* (based on the police force of the same name).

Hungry and destitute, Turpin was all ears when one of his shadier acquaintances suggested that he should try a different, much easier way of making money – as a charity mugger, or, in eighteenth-century parlance, a 'dick'. The next evening, Turpin visited an inn in the dingiest part of the East End, where, after knocking on a hidden door, he exchanged his last few pennies for a brightly coloured waterproof jacket and a clipboard – then, he crept away from his old life and into the night.

News of the new vagabond on the block quickly spread throughout London.

On Tuesday night last, reported the *Weekly Journal* in February 1735, *a dick in a gaudy blue waterproof garment approached Dr Samuel Johnson near his lodgings in Soho and enquired how he was doing that evening and whether he had five minutes. When Mr Johnson ignored him and carried on, the dick obstinately stepped into his path and informed him that he could surely spare just five minutes for some orphans. But being in a great hurry to meet Mr Boswell, Mr Johnson said that he could not, whereupon the dick gave chase with clipboard and pen imploring that the orphans suffered greatly from pleurisy and that the Direct Debit could be cancelled at any time and, when Mr Johnson remained steadfastly silent, the dick was heard to wish him an agreeable night in tones most sarcastic.*

The legend of 'Dick' Turpin was born. Turpin took to his new career like a duck to water. Every Londoner going about his business dreaded the cry of 'Stand and deliver!' and the spectre of Turpin leaping out with his clipboard and his famous pen, a wicked-looking ballpoint known as Black Bess. No man was safe, whether he was eating his lunch, promenading with a lady or pretending to look at something in the other direction. London was a city plagued by dicks in their blue waterproofs but Turpin was a breed apart. Before long, Londoners had had enough and the mayor ordered the Bow Street Runners dispatched to apprehend the blue-clad spectre.

Six of the elite thief-takers made straight for Turpin's haunts in the West End; however, they all returned later that night in various states of confusion. Turpin had cornered one man and persuaded him to sign over six shillings a month for the Royal Hospital at Greenwich. Another man had been trapped in a coffee shop for six hours while Turpin waited outside. A third shamefacedly admitted that he had been powerless to resist signing the dreaded form after Turpin managed to make eye contact from a full three hundred yards away, while a burly sergeant sobbed as he recounted how Turpin had leapt four lanes of moving traffic to ask him if he was having a nice day and whether he had heard about the disgraceful treatment meted out to foxes in the countryside.

The chief and founder of the Bow Street Runners, Henry Fielding, had heard enough. He picked up a newspaper and marched to Leicester Square to purchase a sandwich for his lunch – a challenge he knew Turpin would not be able to resist. It had begun to rain and the narrow streets were deserted. Suddenly, Fielding felt a presence behind him, and sure enough soon came the roar of 'Stand and deliver!' The battle was on.

Fielding was swift: as he saw the clipboard flash in front of him, he ducked, rolled and countered with a firm apology before walking steadily onwards. Turpin was now on the back foot, but quick as a flash he caught up with Fielding and enquired whether he knew how much a donation of just five shillings per month could help a retired horse.

'I already give to three charities,' blurted Fielding.

'Which ones?' enquired the cunning Turpin.

'The Society for Stricken Beggars,' shouted Fielding, pressing boldly on. 'And Scrofulaid! And…' he gasped, but Turpin's piercing gaze was too strong. Fielding's resolve began to ebb from his body.

'And?' said Turpin, waving a picture of an emaciated horse. Try as he might, Fielding could not take his eyes off the horse. It looked horrid. Fielding's legs felt weak. He saw Turpin reach into his pocket and bring out the dreaded Black Bess. With a great marshalling of all of his strength, he roared, 'The Royal Society for the Incarceration of Lunatics at the Bedlam Hospital!', and made a grab for Black Bess. The men struggled, kicking and grasping, but Turpin was the stronger man and he forced the sharp pen up to Fielding's throat.

'Stop!' gasped Fielding. 'I have an idea! My cousin is a well-known theatre producer, and...'

The disappearance of Dick Turpin was the talk of London for many months and, although people initially thought he was simply laying low, he never returned to trouble them. That said, in later years, one or two people would remark on the similarity in appearance between the infamous rogue and the handsome stage actor Titch Rurpin, star of the long-running theatrical drama *The Bow Street Runners*.

DR JOHNSON'S ONLINE ENCYCLOPAEDIA

A S WELL AS HER MILITARY AND ECONOMIC PROWESS, eighteenth-century England had something else to be proud of: her brand new dictionary. The esteemed journalist and man of letters Dr Samuel Johnson had recently compiled a volume of definitions of every single word in the English language – a work of scholarship that had made waves throughout Europe and made Johnson the most celebrated man in all London. The king himself had been so pleased that he had awarded Johnson the sum of a thousand pounds.

Johnson's career had been a meteoric rise to glory. He had come from impoverished beginnings as a bookbinder to be first a teacher, then a magazine writer and poet before spending nine long years writing his dictionary. Then he became bored and began to look around for his next project. It wasn't long before he found it. News arrived from France that the French were compiling the world's first online encyclopaedia: a compendium of all knowledge accessible via the Internet. For the French to achieve such a thing would be a disgrace to English academics, as they all knew that the French would write all manner of rudeness in the 'England' entry. Samuel knew he was the man to beat France at its own game.

He went to the bank, withdrew a portion of his thousand pounds and purchased a wooden laptop, then trotted home and got online. After several hours of looking at pornography and laughing at pictures of silly cats, he made a cup of tea and started work.

Several months later, Johnson emerged from his house very pleased with himself, for his project was well under way. After meeting his pal James Boswell for a few glasses of port at a local tavern, Johnson invited Boswell back to view his creation. Boswell began by typing in the name of Dr Johnson himself. When they viewed the page, however, Johnson was aghast. Instead of reading:

Samuel Johnson (or Dr Johnson), born September 1709, is the pre-eminent author of his age and most famous for compiling a magnificent dictionary of the English language.

the first line now read:

Samuel DONGson (or Dr BENT), born September 1066, is the prICK author of his age and most GAY for compiling a magnificent dicK of GAY SEX.

The online encyclopaedia had been sabotaged. After Boswell had left, giggling, Johnson angrily sat down and traced the identity of the vandal. It was as he thought: the IP address belonged to the Académie Française, France's premier institution of learning. Samuel was incensed. 'I'll show them,' he thought, and he brought up the encyclopaedia page on the Academie and began making some edits of his own. When he was done, the opening paragraph read:

L'Académie Française, or the French KISSING OTHER MEN Academy, is an academic SEXY body considered to be the ultimate autWhorEity on the French language, particularly Tits grammar and its voCRABSulary. It was establishITed in 1635 by Cardinal Richelieu, the chief minGer to Louis XIII.

'That will teach them,' Johnson smirked, and he retired to bed after spending several hours looking at porn.

For the next year, Samuel laboured on his encyclopaedia every day and every night. He got through vast amounts of coffee and racked up several weeks of pornography viewing and, at times, he felt like his work would never be complete. Then, one day, after finishing the entry for 'zoophilia' with the line 'and it is a FACT that members of the Académie Française engage in the practise a hundred per cent of the time', he realized that there was nothing more to write.

News quickly got around about Johnson's achievement and it wasn't long before he was invited to the palace to give a demonstration to the king, who had particularly enjoyed chuckling at the swear words in Johnson's dictionary. Samuel's heart began to race. If the king had awarded him a thousand pounds for a mere dictionary, how much would he shell out for the world's first online encyclopaedia? But then he began to panic. What if the Academie were to get wind of his big day and ruin it somehow?

The day before he was due at the palace, Johnson sat in his study, obsessively checking for signs of vandalism and polishing the highly complimentary entry that he had already written for the king. He stayed up most of the night checking for mischief until he eventually dozed off in his chair.

The next morning, he arrived at the palace with much pomp and glory, proudly bearing his laptop under his arm. The king received him cordially and, in front of the assembled court, requested a demonstration of Johnson's masterpiece. Samuel showed the king how to enter a search term, and, much to Johnson's glee, the first thing the king typed in was his own name. However, when the king began reading the entry, his face darkened with anger and his hands began to shake. Johnson looked down and saw that the first line of the article, which he had written as:

George II of Great Britain is the most magnificent ruler that this country has ever had and is particularly renowned for the generosity with which he rewards humble scholars and encyclopaedia writers.

now read:

George II of Great Britain is the most magnificent TOOL.

'Johnson!' bellowed the king. 'What is the meaning of this?'

Horrified, Johnson realized that the Académie had sabotaged the page. He fell to his knees and began to beg for his life.

'Your Majesty,' he stammered. 'The Académie Française… vandalism… I don't know what has happened, sir!'

'I do,' said the king. 'You've misspelled "has" as "is". What sort of bloody dictionary writer are you? Correct it at once, you useless fool.'

With trembling fingertips, Johnson did as he was told and altered the text to read:

George II of Great Britain HAS the most magnificent TOOL.

'That's better,' the king grunted. 'I must say the whole thing's a pretty childish effort, Johnson. But that's the Internet for you. My wife keeps sending me videos of an animated cat that plays the piano. Anyway – off you go.'

'Bugger,' muttered Johnson as he trudged his way back from the palace with his laptop. He went home and fell asleep after several hours of viewing pornography.

NELSON'S SHOWBIZ COLUMN

WHEN ENGLAND FOUGHT FRANCE IN THE REIGN OF
George III, there was no greater hero than Lord
Horatio Nelson. He first went to sea when he was just twelve
years old but he was brave and clever and rose through the
ranks to become first a captain of the Royal Navy and then an
admiral in charge of the whole fleet. In one battle, he lost an
eye; in another, an arm was shot away.

Now England was embroiled in the Napoleonic Wars and,
as Napoleon of France set his eyes on the ultimate prize of
London, Nelson was her best chance of survival. Despite all of
this, Nelson's real passion was not naval warfare. It was tabloid
journalism.

Nothing gave Nelson greater pleasure than getting hold of the mucky details of a celeb's love life and revealing them in the showbiz column that he wrote for the *London Daily Mercury*. Already renowned for his prowess in battle, he was also the talk of London for obtaining pictures of the voluptuous supermodel Fanny Montague snorting laudanum at a poetry reading and for exposing the Earl of Darrenday as a serial love rat.

In 1805, he was on the tail of a bigger prize. The Duchess of Winemansion, England's most controversial aristocrat and entertainer, had gone missing after a high-profile bust-up with her on-off boyfriend Screaming Lord Blake and England was paralyzed with speculation as to her whereabouts. Nothing had been heard of her for weeks. It was a mystery fit for the most skilled muckracking journalist of the age – and Nelson decided to solve it and reveal all in his column.

Luckily, the navy had just called Nelson back to London to discuss striking a decisive blow against France. That evening, he was received by King George himself, wined, dined and treated to a hero's reception at the palace. Later on, he gave his adoring crowds the slip, changed into a refuse sweeper's uniform and headed up to Camden to strike a blow of his own. Stealthily, he crept into the Duchess of Winemansion's garden, quietly emptied her dustbins onto the lawn and rooted through the contents until he found what he was looking for.

The next day, Nelson arrived back at navy headquarters with a plan of action.

'Gentlemen,' he announced. 'We will strike the French off Cape Trafalgar, near the Spanish town of Cadiz.'

'Are you sure, sir?' said Admiral Cornwallis. 'The coast is treacherous there. There's little in the area but long, sandy beaches.'

'Yes,' said Nelson, grinning. 'Yes indeed.'

The next day, Nelson hopped into his battleship, *HMS Victory*, and set out for Trafalgar at the head of an entire fleet. *Victory* was equipped with a hundred guns capable of dealing death from all angles, as well as with telephoto lenses capable of capturing an exposed nipple from a thousand yards away. She was backed up by thirty ships, all of them teeming with bloodthirsty sailors and marines. After several days of sailing, they arrived at the beach of Trafalgar to find a vast line of French ships sailing up the coast in the direction of England.

'What is the plan of attack, my lord?' asked Nelson's faithful captain Thomas Hardy. 'May I suggest that we wait until evening and attack in a parallel line formation?'

'We will go at them from the side now, Hardy,' Nelson said, 'punching through their line and heading for the beach.'

'We'll be smashed to smithereens, sir,' said Hardy. 'A victory will be impossible. And why do we want to get to the beach?'

'Hardy,' said Nelson. 'I am after a far bigger prize than victory today.'

'The immortality of a place in history?' said Hardy.

'Don't be a pompous arse,' said Nelson. 'I'm going to get the dirt on the Duchess of Winemansion. She's sunning herself right now – probably topless – on the beach at Cape Trafalgar with a mystery man!'

'This is madness, sir,' retorted Hardy.

'Is it hell,' Nelson cried. 'I found the travel agent's receipt in her dustbin!'

'But sir…' said Hardy.

'The curious public's appetite for showbiz scandal must be fed at all costs,' cried Nelson. 'Make ready the telephoto lenses! And get the signalling flags out – I need to write an inspiring message to the fleet!'

Hardy got out the flags, swearing under his breath, and Nelson duly arranged them so that they spelled out:

'England Expects Pop Stunner In Beach Romp Shocker!'

A great cheer went up from the English sailors and the English fleet crashed into the French line with a thundering roar of cannon fire.

The battle was long and hard. Grapeshot and cannonballs tore the air and men fought hand to hand with cutlasses and camera tripods. Nelson's *HMS Victory* was in the middle of the fray, surrounded by French ships and raked by gunfire on all sides.

Suddenly, the shout went up from the crow's nest that the duchess had turned up on the beach to watch the battle, dressed in nothing but a bikini. Slashing left and right with his cutlass, Nelson shinned up the mast with his camera strap in his teeth. He aimed his camera and howled with all his might for the Duchess of Winemansion to give him a smile.

When she realized that she was being addressed by the hero of England, she sprang to her feet, letting her bikini top fall to the ground.

'Paydirt!' roared Nelson, clicking away with his camera. 'Winemansion in beachside nip slip!'

At that very moment, a French sniper took aim and fired at Nelson. The musketball passed right through his telephoto lens and into his brain and he fell to the deck with a thud. Hardy came running and stood over the dying admiral.

'Send the pictures,' Nelson hissed weakly.

'I will, sir,' said the tearful Hardy. 'I'll have them couriered to the picture desk of the *Daily Mercury* at once. You will be on the front page, my lord.'

'Spoken like a true tabloid journalist,' said Nelson. 'Kiss me, Hardy'.

'Hmm…' said Hardy.

The next day, Nelson was indeed on the front of the *London Daily Mercury*.

'NELSON COMES OUT ON DEATHBED,' read the headline. 'REAR ADMIRAL EXPECTS THAT EVERY MAN WILL DO HIS BOOTY. By new star reporter Thomas Hardy.'

WEBB ELLIS INVENTS A NEW GAME

URING THE NINETEENTH CENTURY, IT WAS THE DONE thing for rich families to send their sons to one of the great public schools of England. The combination of learning, team sports and flogging helped to shape many of our greatest statesmen and generals, as well as turning out some less likely heroes.

One such figure was William Webb Ellis, a pupil of Rugby school. One wet and rainy day, he and his classmates were out on the football field and the game was going particularly badly for him. Not only had he been whacked on the back of the legs by a wet, muddy ball several times but the various housemasters' daughters were playing badminton in the gym and he very much wanted to go in there and stare at them in their revealing PE kits. As a sliding tackle from behind sent him tumbling into the mud yet again, he thought of an ingenious ruse to get himself sent indoors to sit with the girls.

The next time the ball rolled towards him, he picked it up and ran. He charged right through his shocked classmates, touched the ball on the goal line at the far end and turned around holding the ball aloft, crying, 'I have committed a most terrible foul! I'm so ashamed that I must resign my place on the team forthwith and go indoors to watch the girls play badminton.'

'That was indeed a vile foul,' said the games master, boiling with rage at the boy's cheek. 'So vile a foul,' he growled, 'that Webb Ellis's entire team are disqualified on the spot. I will now turn my back for a full minute while they conduct a post-match analysis with him.'

'Oh dear,' said William Webb Ellis as fourteen boys leapt on him and began to beat him quite severely. But he was a slippery character, and he fought, gouged, bit and twisted, and although his attackers had hold of his clothes he managed to extricate himself by wriggling out of them. He fled, quite naked, across the pitch, still holding the ball. A roar went up and his classmates gave pursuit.

William could have taken his beating there and then, but he was a spirited lad. Seeing the school wall ahead, he took a giant run-up and managed to clamber right over it. He ran for his life, still holding the ball, down the road towards the town of Rugby itself – only to look behind him when he got there to see that his disgruntled teammates were still on his tail.

In desperation, he decided on a shortcut through the local brewery – but it turned out to be a dead end. With his pursuers closing on him, he leapt into a vat of half-fermented beer and submerged himself in it. He stayed there for several minutes, swallowing a great deal of beer and fermenting hops by accident, then he clambered out again and attempted to sneak home – but he heard a shout from behind him and the chase was on again.

Perhaps because of all the beer he had swallowed – or perhaps in spite of it – Webb Ellis ran faster this time and managed to make it all the way to the centre of Rugby. Naked, soaked in beer and clutching the football, he dashed through the nearest doorway, which was the entrance to an upmarket hotel, with his pursuers hot on his heels as he sprinted through the corridors.

With seconds to spare before they caught him, he bolted for the lavatories and locked himself in a cubicle, where he held his

breath as his pursuers clattered into the room looking for him. He might have got away with it but for the amount of half-fermented beer that he'd swallowed, which caused his stomach to growl loudly. A yell went up and his teammates began hammering on the door. In a state of panic, the now-drunk Webb Ellis scrambled over the cubicle wall, catching the end of the loo roll in his buttocks as he thrashed his legs desperately.

With six feet of loo roll now trailing behind him, William skidded out of the lavatories, naked, steaming drunk and still clutching the football. He barged through a set of double doors in front of him and, to his horror, now found himself in the hotel's busy restaurant. The shocked diners stared, aghast, and one gentleman spat his soup out.

As the mob closed in on him, Webb Ellis decided there was nothing else for it but to keep running. He charged through the restaurant, vaulting a table and accidentally lighting the end of the loo roll on a candle. His stomach was growling now from the sour hops he'd swallowed. With fear of his classmates driving him on, William cleared the last of the diners and ran through another door. He was now in the hotel bar and it was a dead end. Webb Ellis was trapped.

Thinking fast, William realized that his only means of escape was to take a running jump at a large, chariot-shaped chandelier that hung above the bar. If he could jump high enough to grab the chandelier, he might be able to swing on it through a small window that opened on to the street and make good his escape. He steeled himself, ran and jumped with all his might.

To his astonishment, he grabbed the chariot-shaped chandelier and began to swing for the window – but the effort caused his stomach to growl more and more violently. He swung harder and harder but the window was out of reach.

'Swing low, sweet chariot!' howled Webb Ellis. At that second, his exertions caused him to break wind violently onto the burning loo roll, which caused a six-foot eruption of blue flame to belch across the room. William let go his grip on the chandelier and fell, naked and scorched, into a table full of drinks, which went over with a crash. The football rolled slowly across the room and came to rest at his teammates' feet.

After some time, the captain of the football team spoke up.

'That was bloody brilliant,' he said. 'I think you've invented a new sport, Webb Ellis.'

'Let's call it Rugby Football!' said another boy.

'I'm next on the chandelier – get me a pint,' said another boy. 'Who's going to light my loo roll for me?'

And thus a great English tradition was invented.

Stephenson's Pimped-Out Rocket

I N 1829, THE VEHICLE THAT WOULD USHER IN THE AGE OF Steam and with it the era of high-speed mass transportation arrived. Its name was the Rocket and it was a locomotive that moved under its own steam along two iron rails. The contraption was invented by the father-and-son team of Robert and George Stephenson.

The Liverpool and Manchester Railway had just been built and the owners decided to hold a competition for engine builders to decide who would manufacture the railway's locomotives. The Stephensons arrived with the Rocket – a fine engine that puffed clouds of smoke and trounced the other entries, many of which broke down. They were awarded the prize of a hundred pounds and the honour of driving the Rocket at the railway's opening ceremony, a star-studded trip from Manchester to Liverpool and back with the Duke of Wellington and several newspaper reporters on board.

'There will also be a special guest of honour,' said the railway's owner, 'the actress Miss Fanny Braithwaite.'

'Fanny Braithwaite?' gasped Robert.

'The hottest piece this side of Paris!' his son George squeaked.

Both Stephensons had had a crush on Fanny Braithwaite ever since she had first appeared as a humble glamour model for the painter Joshua Reynolds. Since then, she had become a star, appearing in her own plays that the Stephensons attended religiously every time she was in town. Now they would be driving her to Liverpool and back in their Rocket.

'I will be honoured to drive the engine that draws Miss Braithwaite's carriage, sir,' said Robert Stephenson, bowing low.

'What my father means, sir, is that he will be honoured to have his son drive the engine,' said George Stephenson, glaring at his dad.

The railway owner decided that it would be wise to leave at this point.

The Stephensons drove the Rocket back home, bickering

all the way about who would drive Fanny Braithwaite. All evening they quarrelled, with each arguing that they had done the greater part of building the Rocket. Robert called his son a disrespectful little tyke and George called his father an egregious old fart. Eventually, Mrs Stephenson rapped them both about the head with a ladle and made them toss a coin to see who would drive the engine. To George's delight, he won the toss and Robert stamped off to bed without saying a word.

George slept fitfully that night and he fancied he heard lots of banging and clattering of metal in his dreams. When he awoke in the morning, his father was nowhere to be seen. He shrugged, had a cup of tea and set off in the Rocket, wondering if he might get a glimpse down the front of Fanny Braithwaite's dress. He rolled up at the opening ceremony and was delighted to see that Miss Braithwaite looked greatly impressed by his engine. He helped her aboard gallantly and prepared to set off. Just then, there was a commotion outside.

To everyone's great surprise, a second Rocket arrived at the railway in a great thundering of cloud and steam, reported Charles Dibthwaite of *The Times. This one was driven by Mr Robert Stephenson, father of Mr George Stephenson, and was similar in appearance except for a large chrome spoiler fixed to the engine's rear as well as a windscreen sticker reading 'Whale*

Oil Beef Hooked', which caused Miss Fanny Braithwaite to giggle coquettishly.

'Hello son,' said Robert with a smile. 'Lovely day for a drive. Miss Braithwaite, would you care to ride in my better-looking Rocket instead? It's got reclining seats, you know.'

'I do like the extras,' simpered Miss Braithwaite, and, to George's horror, she climbed across into the cab of Robert's engine. 'Sorry, George,' she said. 'I'm a sucker for a bad boy with wheels.'

'See you later, loser,' Robert cackled, and he set out for Liverpool at the grand speed of eight miles per hour. George was incensed. He set off in hot pursuit, then stopped, reversed, parked his Rocket and ran into a nearby scrapyard. For the next hour, he ran back and forth with pieces of metal, and a great deal of banging came from inside the Rocket's cab, which caused George's passengers to wonder what was going on. At last, George blew the Rocket's whistle and the train set off – at an amazingly high speed.

A furious din followed as the train pulled away and sped up with a roar, wrote Dibthwaite. *All in the carriage were flung backwards into their seats as the Rocket thundered along the track at a frightening rate. Several elderly ladies swooned. It was as if we were on a ride to Hell. A terrible thumping music began to emit from the Rocket as well as clouds of smoke. The Duke of Wellington evacuated the contents of his stomach all down his frock coat, and we clung to the windows with white knuckles, fearing for our very lives.*

George had pimped his Rocket to the max. He had blacked out every window of the cab and installed a violently loud gramophone with speakers that caused the whole carriage to shake under the force of a thumping bassline. He had also installed a turbo charger in the engine, replaced the wheels with nineteen-inch alloys and the chimney with a large-bore twin exhaust pipe. George's rocket flew along at forty-five miles per hour. His passengers were screaming for him to stop, but his father's engine was in sight.

'How do you like this, Father?' yelled George as his Rocket drew level. 'Perhaps, Miss Braithwaite, you would prefer to ride in this beast?'

'What an impressive engine!' cried Miss Braithwaite. 'Can I be in charge of the tunes?'

'Yes, and you can stoke my engine!' yelled George. The actress skilfully hopped out of Robert's train and into George's and they soon left Robert for dust.

George Stephenson's Rocket reached Liverpool in record time. His passengers were dishevelled, shaken and could barely stand. The Duke of Wellington was last to get to his feet. Drawing his sword, he attempted to enter the cab of the Rocket but found it locked. As he hammered on the door, he realized that the engine was rocking gently from side to side. This was too much for the duke and he ran into the new railway station howling for the police.

After some time, the door of the Rocket swung open and Miss Fanny Braithwaite stepped out, smoking a cigarette, followed by George Stephenson, who looked mightily pleased with himself. After some time, Robert's Rocket came puffing down the track and pulled into the railway station. Both father and son glared at each other for some time. But suddenly the two men burst out laughing at the ridiculous turn of events, clapped each other on the back and climbed into George's ultra-pimped Rocket and sped all the way home with smiles on their faces.

Neither Stephenson was ever invited to an opening ceremony again. The Duke of Wellington made an official complaint and the pair were disgraced. They didn't mind, however: the engineering geniuses were far too busy driving their pimped Rockets up and down Blackpool seafront, looking cool, doing wheel spins and picking up chicks.

CHARLES DICKENS AND JAMIE OLIVER TWIST

W HEN VICTORIAN CHILDREN WERE FINISHED WITH their homework and chores for the day, they loved nothing more than to hear their father read to them from one of the popular novels of the day – and there was no novel more popular than Charles Dickens' *Jamie Oliver Twist*. The story of an orphan who dreamed of becoming a celebrity chef, the book is considered Dickens' masterpiece and remains a firm favourite to this day.

The story begins with little Jamie Oliver Twist born into happy circumstances in the Home Counties. His parents were talented and prosperous high-society chefs who wrote their own best-selling cookbooks and lived off a healthy diet of organic foodstuffs grown in their beautiful kitchen garden. Sadly, one day his parents were gored to death by a rampant British Saddleback organic sow on heat and the young Jamie was left all alone in the world.

He was sent to the dreaded workhouse, which is where waifs and strays ended up in those days. There, he was put to work with a hundred other boys who spent their days performing menial labour and eating cheap, processed food. The workhouse was run to a tight budget and its dinners were notoriously low in nutrients and full of empty calories. Particularly bad was the microwaved gruel, a single serving of which contained ten grams of sugar and a full sixty per cent of an orphan's recommended daily salt intake.

One night, young Jamie Oliver Twist declared that the next day he would walk up to the master after supper and ask for a healthier alternative. The boys scorned him, for they thoroughly enjoyed their evening meal of gruel and chips, but Jamie was resolved to make a stand.

The next day, the gruel and chips were dished out and a long grace was said. The children went to work on their plates until they were licked clean. With all eyes on him, Jamie rose from his seat, desperate from the added salt and reckless with processed sugar. He advanced to the master, stylish white bowl and spoon in hand, and said:

'Please, me old china, may I 'ave something less salty?'

The master was a fat, healthy man, but he turned very pale. He gazed in stupefied astonishment at the lovable scamp for some seconds, and then clung for support to the gruel oven.

'What?!' said the master at length, in a faint voice.

'Please, sir,' replied Jamie Oliver Twist, 'this is well unhealthy, innit. I could knock up a pucka broccoli en croute drizzled with salmon jus in half the time you took to make this shit, pardon me old French.'

The master aimed a blow at Jamie's flapping tongue with the ladle and shrieked aloud for the beadle. Jamie grabbed the ladle and produced a leek from his pocket.

'Look 'ere,' he said, 'we just quarter this leek, well easy innit, and smack its bitch up with this shittin' ladle. Bish bash bosh, chuck it in a pre-heated oven and my old maaaan said follow the vaaan.'

Mr Bumble looked at the boy, aghast, and then rushed into the workhouse boardroom in great excitement.

'Mr Limbkins, I beg your pardon, sir!' he said to the gentleman at the head of the table. 'Jamie Oliver Twist has begun a campaign for healthier workhouse dinners and is talking seditious gibberish!'

'Healthier dinners?' said Mr Limbkins. 'Do I understand that he asked for healthier dinners, after consuming his gruel?'

'He did, sir,' replied Bumble. 'He has threatened to run away to London to tell the prime minister that our gruel contains just fifty per cent real gruel and the rest is water, fat, colourings, flavourings and additives. And he called me a dopey plum!'

'That boy will be hung!' said the gentleman in the white waistcoat.

'No I fackin' won't,' shouted Oliver, bursting into the room, whirling an organic chicken around his head. 'I shall have a celebrity lifestyle and several shows, an advertising deal with a major food retailer AND my own rock band.'

'That's it,' said Mr Bumble. 'Fetch that chimney sweep who was looking for an assistant.'

'Bugger it,' said Jamie, quietly. 'I shall never taste another sun-dried tomato now.'

Jamie was bundled out of the workhouse and apprenticed to a vile old chimney sweep named Mr Gamfield who sent him up chimneys all day, every day, and – worse still – fed the lad nothing but great quantities of cheap, processed gruel with mountains of chips and gallons of fizzy pop. The poor boy soon grew terribly chubby and it wasn't long before he began to get stuck in people's chimneys. Nobody wanted a small boy stuck in their chimney – especially one who kept going on about additives and E numbers while Mr Gamfield tried to push him out with his broom and trod soot all over the house.

One day, while stuck up such a chimney and being poked cruelly from below by Mr Gamfield's chimney brush, Jamie wriggled and wriggled until he popped out of the chimney. Quick as a flash, he shinned down a drainpipe and ran away to London. There, his life took a happier turn when he fell in with a gang of pickpockets who pilfered organic fruit and veg from Borough Market and carried it away to a gleaming minimalist kitchen in the East End to share amongst themselves.

Eventually, he would set up his own restaurant staffed entirely by former chimney sweeps and frequented by the rich and famous – and even Queen Victoria herself was known to visit Jamie Oliver Twist's establishment for a bowl of his finest chimney-smoked artichoke gruel.

As for Twist's creator, Charles Dickens went on to write many more celebrated novels about young, aspiring chefs until, in 1860, he overstepped the bounds of good taste with the expletive-riddled *Gordon Fucking Copperfield* and was asked politely to stop.

THE CHARGE OF THE LIGHT BRIGADE

Sofas to right of them
Bedsteads to left of them
Meatballs behind them
Bargains they plundered

(TENNYSON)

THE CRIMEAN WAR (1853–56) WAS A TERRIBLE CONTEST between the major powers of Europe over the territories of the declining Ottoman Empire, and the English were up to their necks in it, fighting in several bloody battles on the Crimean Peninsula of modern-day Ukraine. However, the worst day of the war occurred away from the battlefield – at the opening of a brand-new furniture store in the city of Sevastopol.

With the Battle of Balaclava raging, the British commander Lord Raglan stood on a hill watching the action unfold beneath him. Both sides had fought for days, hurling themselves at each other in an unremitting, bloody slaughter.

But now he saw the Russians abandoning their posts and heading away from the battlefield towards Sevastopol *en masse*. Thinking he was watching a British victory, Raglan leapt up from his chair and called for an aide to tell him what was going on.

'It's the new Ikea, sir,' said the aide, doffing his hat.

'What?!' Raglan exclaimed.

'It's a store that sells excellently priced and tasteful furniture and household goods,' said the aide. 'You do have to assemble it yourself, but…'

'I know what a bloody Ikea is,' Raglan barked. 'Mrs Raglan has me trailing around the Croydon one every bloody Saturday. What I want to know is why the Russians are abandoning their posts for this?'

'They're after the discount, sir,' said the admonished aide. 'It's fifty per cent on all sofas and lighting for one day only, starting in half an hour. The enemy will get all the best bargains, sir.'

'Bastards,' murmured Raglan. 'The black-hearted bastards.'

Lord Raglan had good reason to be angry. For months and months, Lady Raglan had been going on about a stylish set of Ikea lamps for the living room. She'd had them circled in the catalogue for some time, and Raglan knew that his first duty when he got home would be to go out and get them. Now here they were, and half price too. If he could get his hands on the lamps, he could avoid a trip to Ikea and save money as well – but surely the Russians would clear off with the lot. He thought for a second and ordered several regiments of cavalry under Lord Cardigan to be brought to him.

Moments later, six hundred of his finest cavalry troops were lined up in front of him and Raglan explained their mission: to beat the Russians to the store opening and return with his wife's lamps at all costs. With a resounding hurrah, the men spurred their horses, drew their swords and set off down the hill towards Sevastopol.

Their first obstacle was the Russian guns at the bottom of the hill half a league away. They thundered the whole way there and charged the guns in a terrible hand-to-hand battle. Many were cut down on both sides as men clashed with sabres and rifle butts and horses squealed in the confusion. Less than half of the 'Light Brigade', as they had now christened themselves, made it past the guns but those who did were even more resolute in their hearts. They galloped on until they reached the city outskirts and eventually found themselves outside the Ikea.

It was closed: someone had blundered – namely Raglan's aide, who had got the opening time wrong. Suddenly, the

Russians arrived on the scene. A second pitched battle broke out as the Light Brigade valiantly defended the entrance against the hordes. Many more men fell dead before the doors finally opened and the two forces surged inside.

At this point, order disintegrated entirely. The British led a valiant sabre charge up the stairs only to find themselves lost in the food hall. Here, the 13th Dragoons demanded that the Brigade stop for meatballs and potatoes with lingonberry sauce on the side, and many men grabbed trays and headed for the food servers. Cardigan was forced to restore order by shooting the ringleaders, and, once again, the Light Brigade surged forth.

Now, they found themselves trapped on a circular route between Kitchens and Dining, which they followed in circles several times while taking heavy enfilading fire from a Russian grenadier regiment positioned behind a bank of pine tables. Several men dismounted to look at chairs and were cut down by a pursuing regiment of Russian cavalry, while Cardigan himself was bayoneted in the thigh after stopping to admire a solid wood wine rack. Many of the troopers were now weighed down by yellow carrier bags full of plates and utensils and it was a greatly depleted Light Brigade that finally broke through into the Living Rooms area – only to find it swarming with the enemy.

With a final desperate battle cry, the Light Brigade spurred their horses into the fray. Steel flashed, shot and shell flew and the store rang with the agonies of the dying. Finally, Cardigan saw the lamps: a regiment of Cossacks was carrying them away. He charged in, sabre flashing right and left, grabbed the lamps and sounded the retreat. The remnants of the Brigade had to fight their way out of the store to the tills, where several men died of their wounds in the queue – but the lamps were theirs.

Of the six hundred men who set out to the Ikea opening, only seven made it back to the British lines with Lord Raglan's lamps. The spectacle prompted the French commander Pierre

Bosquet to famously comment, 'C'est de la folie – mais c'est une bonne affaire': it is madness, but what a bargain.

Many months later, it was with a heavy heart that Raglan disembarked in London and carried the precious lamps home to his wife.

'Thank you ever so much, my darling,' she said, clutching him tight. 'But I got tired of waiting for them so I went and purchased a set by mail order. You'll have to take these ones back. But… I saved the treat of assembling them for you.'

Lord Raglan took out his screwdriver like a broken man and went to work.